The Natural Arches
of the Big South Fork

The

Natural
Arches

of the

Outdoor Tennessee Series
Jim Casada, Series Editor

Big South Fork

A Guide to Selected Landforms

Arthur McDade

The University of Tennessee Press / Knoxville

Frontispiece and Part 2 division page: Natural Arch, Daniel Boone National Forest. Photograph by Arthur McDade. *Part 1 division page:* Blue Heron Mine Tipple. Photograph by Arthur McDade.

 The Outdoor Tennessee Series covers a wide range of topics of interest to the general reader, including titles on the flora and fauna, the varied recreational activities, and the rich history of outdoor Tennessee. With a keen appreciation of the importance of protecting our state's natural resources and beauty, the University of Tennessee Press intends the series to emphasize environmental awareness and conservation.

Library of Congress Cataloging-in-Publication Data

McDade, Arthur, 1950–
The natural arches of the Big South Fork : a guide to selected landforms / Arthur McDade. — 1st ed.
p. cm. — (Outdoor Tennessee series)
Includes bibliographical references (p.   ) and index.
ISBN 1-57233-074-0 (pbk. : alk. paper)
1. Hiking—Big South Fork National River and Recreation Area (Tenn. and Ky.) Guidebooks. 2. Natural history—Big South Fork National River and Recreation Area (Tenn. and Ky.) Guidebooks. 3.Trails—Big South Fork National River and Recreation Area (Tenn. and Ky.) Guidebooks. 4. Big South Fork National River and Recreation Area (Tenn. and Ky.) Guidebooks. I. Title. II. Series.
GV199.42.B55 M39 2000
917.68'71—dc21
99-6687

For Mother and, in memory, Dad
For Nathan, Mallory, Molly, Dennis,
Rebecca, Pat, and Ted

CONTENTS

ILLUSTRATIONS

Figures

Maps

EDITOR'S FOREWORD

Rocks and rock formations have always fascinated humanity. From a practical perspective, rocks served early humans in a wide variety of ways. Caves, overhanging cliff faces, ledges, and other natural retreats provided shelter from the elements and a safe haven from enemies. Certain types of rocks offered the magic of fire, that discovery which set humans apart from other creatures. Stones served as weapons in such diverse forms as arrowheads and spearheads, clubs, and missiles to be thrown or slung. In this context, the symbolism found in the biblical story of David and Goliath, where a stone and a sling in the right hands defy dramatic odds, is noteworthy. Many primitive tools were likewise fashioned from rocks—nutting stones, mortar and pestle to grind grain, and the like. Nor should the uses of stone as a building material, beginning with the transition from a nomadic lifestyle to a settled existence, and continuing to the present day, be overlooked.

Turning from practical uses to the ways stones can stir the soul and give rise to enduring visions, it takes little in the way of visualizing to realize how prominently rocks—whether vast geologic formations or a small pebble worn smooth by countless eons of water flow—figure in the human imagination. Who does not recall, from the halcyon days of youth, carefully selecting flat rocks to skip on water? Or what rural image, at least in the hills and hollows of the Tennessee high country, is more enduring than a lad with a pocket full of rocks perfectly suited as missiles for a handcrafted slingshot made of a Y-forked piece of dogwood, a patch of soft leather, and strips from an old inner tube?

Then too, we must remember the silent stones which serve as mute but memorable sentinels to a way of life in a world we have lost. In their various forms and manifestations, they greet observant, knowing wayfarers who walk the hills. Sometimes these stones stand forlorn and forgotten in small cemeteries cloaking the points of rounded knobs and finger ridges. In other locations they form rambling fence rows in coves where families once eked out a hardscrabble living as subsistence farmers, line creek banks alongside abandoned fields, or mark the outline of spring houses where milk and butter were once stored.

Yet it is the rock shaped and crafted by nature's patient hands, not those moved and improved by people, which sends our imaginations soaring and gives birth to verbal flights of fancy. One needs only think of place names from most anywhere in Appalachia to realize how deeply our forebears were impressed by outstanding geologic features and how gifted these simple folk were when it came to power of description. Names which spring immediately to my mind, a reflection of being a staunch son of the Great Smokies, include Charlie's Bunion, Chimney Rock, the Chimneys, Shining Rock, Slickrock Creek, Sliding Rock, Rocky Top, Rock Fork, and many more. A particular personal favorite, as forlorn a testament to a down-and-out location somewhere on the other side of nowhere as one could possibly imagine, is Stoney Lonesome.

All of the above-mentioned locations are ones I know well, whether in song ("Rocky Top") or from first-hand experience. When it comes to pure visual grandeur, though, all of them pale by comparison with the geologic wonders provided by natural arches. Doubtless that was one reason every school kid (at least of my generation) was familiar with Virginia's Natural Bridge, often touted as one of the "Seven Natural Wonders of the World." Sadly, this particular example of nature's handicraft has been overly commercialized and surrounded by sufficient tawdriness and tackiness to qualify for the designation "tourist trap."

Such is not the case in the arches and other geological features covered in this book. They thankfully remain little troubled by commercialization or the gimmickry and greed we too frequently associate with the beauty provided us by the good earth. Indeed, as the work makes clear, the region in which these geologic features are found constitutes a special sort of conservation success story, one in which the unkindest of human ravages are gradually being erased by nature's healing balm in the form of reforestation and increasingly clean waters. That consideration alone suffices to nestle this work squarely into the thrust of the Outdoor Tennessee series of which it becomes a welcome part, and it is my firm conviction that all who read it and visit the region it describes will leave *The Natural Arches of the Big South Fork* with an enhanced appreciation of the importance which attaches to protecting and perpetuating the wonders of the wild world.

In the pages which follow you will encounter not one but several natural bridges or arches, all of which are a far and welcome cry from the one found alongside Interstate 81 in Virginia. Likewise, there is coverage of other arches and landforms with captivating and intriguing names such as Hidden Passage, Yahoo Arch, Robber's Roost, Dwarf Arch, and Cracks-in-the-Roof. All these, and a score more, are located in the Big South Fork (of the Cumberland River) National River and Recreation Area, Daniel Boone National Forest, or Pickett State Park. Most are readily accessible, requiring only a short hike from a road, but a few are so remote as to defy visits by any but the fit and hardy. However, the basic thrust and scope of the work is, in the author's words, "focused on the most significant arches and features that are generally accessible to a visitor to the Big South Fork area with a moderate amount of effort and with no specialized equipment." In other words, this is a practical guidebook intended for use by the average individual, and to my way of thinking that is precisely as it should be. However, those who are more adventurous or like their exposure to nature in especially remote areas will find tidbits here which likely will tempt them to explore further.

All the natural features covered in this book form part of the upland region of eastern Tennessee and southeastern Kentucky known as the Northern Cumberland Plateau. Local folks have always called it Big South Fork Country, and a rugged, remote, and lovely country it is. It is truly plateau country, intersected by the river's deeply gouged gorge, and the sandstone which constitutes most of the region is soft enough to lend itself to shaping and sculpting, carving and crafting, at the hands of water and wind, rain and ice.

The area is one which Arthur McDade, the author of the book, has known and loved for upwards of two decades. A park ranger in the Big South Fork Area, McDade has visited and worked in the area for some time. For all its wildness and sense of the remote, the region is also surprisingly small. Encompassing only 200,000 acres or so, the Big South Fork nonetheless manages to give the visitor a feeling of being, in the words so cherished by that sage of the nearby Great Smokies, Horace Sowers Kephart, "back of beyond." Once visitors have seen and savored the visual wonders of the region, though, they may well decide that a more apt description would be that favored by another regional writer, Leroy Sossamon, who entitled one of his works *The Backside of Heaven.*

This guidebook—and for all its skillful crafting and easy flow that is what it is—takes the reader by the hand in a most pleasing fashion. We begin with an overview of the Big South Fork Area and then delve somewhat more deeply into the land, the river, and the humans (Native Americans and the settlers who largely supplanted them) who have lived there. We soon learn that, for all its contemporary appearance of wildness, the area has not always been so. Indeed, it was only after lumbering and coal-mining operations ceased, with resultant reforestation and a cessation in siltation and acid runoff, that this part of the Cumberland Plateau was gradually able to shake off the singularly unkind attention accorded it in the late nineteenth and early twentieth centuries.

McDade makes all of this clear and in so doing provides a suitable backdrop for the heart of the book—the geologic features of the Big South Fork. With helpful guidance from maps and illustrations, the reader is introduced to carefully selected geologic high points. In each instance detailed directions are provided, complete with distances, information on parking, comments on readily noticeable landmarks along the way, and the like. The arches, bridges, and other individual geologic features are likewise described in full.

There is vicarious pleasure in perusing these pages, but their real impact comes with the growing realization that an inner voice is telling you: "I don't just want to read about these places; I want to go there." To do so, with Arthur McDade as your guide, is to tread paths of first literary then geologic wonder. There is something about the Big South Fork area which mesmerizes and mystifies, and—whether by accident or design—the author concludes with precisely the right touch when he speaks of "a sense of magic and wonder in these hills." The only way to relish these senses to the fullest degree is to go there, and should you join the growing number of visitors who come to enjoy solitude and splendor, I urge you to do so with this book as a companion in your backpack or daypack. You will find it a fine and trusty companion.

Jim Casada
Series Editor
Rock Hill, South Carolina

DIRECTIONS AND DESCRIPTIONS

The directions to all the features in this guide begin at one of the two National Park Service (NPS) visitor centers in the Big South Fork National River and Recreation Area (BSFNRRA). The NPS visitor center in Tennessee is called Bandy Creek and is located twelve miles west of Oneida, Tennessee, off Tennessee Highway 297. The Kentucky visitor center is located in Stearns, Kentucky, a short distance over the Tennessee-Kentucky state line on Highway 92. Unless otherwise indicated, routes to the geological features on the west side of the Big South Fork River in Tennessee, as well as Chimney Rocks at Station Camp, begin at Bandy Creek. Routes to those features in Kentucky generally take the Kentucky visitor center as their starting point, unless otherwise noted. Each landform description identifies the starting point. Mileage from the starting point to the destination is approximate, since motor vehicle odometers vary. The mileage readings of your motor vehicle may differ by several tenths of a mile from those given in this guide.

I have tried to arrange the arch descriptions so that the reader can visit as many landform features as possible in a given outing. In some cases, as in Pickett State Park, this was easy to do. In Pickett, the landforms are close together and can be reached conveniently from a paved road, Tennessee Highway 154; I have even included a connector trail description linking five different landforms. An energetic and physically fit hiker could visit all the Pickett features in one day, or certainly in one weekend. Several of the landforms in and around the BSFNRRA also lend themselves to being visited in one outing (assuming physical fitness and sufficient time). Split Bow Arch, New Arch, Wagon Arch, and Cracks-in-the-Rock are all reasonably accessible in one outing, as are Dead Deer Arch, Needle Arch, and Slave Falls. The arches in the Daniel Boone National Forest, however, are not so conveniently arranged. Most of them are located on gravel U.S. Forest Service roads, and these may or may not display definite route numbers. It can be very difficult to provide clear directions to landforms located on obscure gravel roads off long, looping routes, particularly if visitors are not familiar with the area. Ultimately, the only simple and safe way to direct readers to some of these remote features is to use an NPS visitor center as the starting point for traveling to each specific feature. Consequently, in this book, the directions to arches are largely linear in nature—that is, they go from starting point to landform destination. In some instances, particularly in the Daniel Boone National Forest, few or no connector directions to other features could be given.

To visit all the landform features identified in this guide will require several outings. It is my belief that these arches and landforms are best savored at a leisurely pace during several visits to the Big South Fork country, rather than bagged at breakneck pace in some geological marathon.

The measurements provided for each landform's height and width are drawn from actual measurements done in the field, as well as prior measurements by government agencies on whose lands the features stand. In the case of the Daniel Boone National Forest, the U.S. Forest Service has compiled a file of arches and waterfalls in the Big South Fork area, giving established measurements. Some of the arch measurements were established earlier by James X. Corgan and John T. Parks in *The Natural Bridges of Tennessee* (see "Selected References"). When no officially established height and width existed for a given landform, I measured it. I used the apex of the arch's lintel as the point under which I took my measurements. Obviously, where I stood underneath the lintel of the arches was a subjective factor, and the next person measuring might stand only a short distance away and get a different measurement, since the character of rock breakdown and of rock litter underneath is uneven. The measurements are as valid as can be gotten manually, without using lasers or other sophisticated electronic measuring devices which are difficult to obtain and haul into the field.

Each arch description contains the name of the appropriate United States Geological Survey (USGS) 7.5-minute topographical map quadrangle, for further geographical reference. However, the USGS maps are limited in that they do not show most of the landform features identified in this guide. Most of the arches and landforms were discovered after the topo maps were drawn; in some cases, extant information about them was overlooked. This book's appendix A, however, contains line maps showing the general location of every landform described. These line maps are general location maps only; they are not drawn to scale, and they are not designed to show topographic features or trail directions or connections. Therefore, I highly recommend buying and referring to the "Trails Illustrated" topographic map of the Big South Fork area, which is published by the National Geographic Society. This map shows all the designated trails in the area. Both the USGS quad maps and the "Trails Illustrated" map can be purchased from the Eastern National Association at the BSFNRRA (see appendix B for address).

A vicinity map and a general location map of the Big South Fork area follow this section. The arch/landform maps are grouped together in appendix A.

There are a couple of hiking guidebooks for the Big South Fork region which can be helpful, especially for readers who want to make longer loop trail connections. They are listed in the "Selected References" section.

For more information on the fascinating natural and cultural resources of this area, write ahead for the National Park Service's free Big South Fork National River and Recreation Area park map and brochure, or pick one up upon arrival. You can request a brochure from both Pickett State Park (ask for their free trail map also) and the Daniel Boone National Forest. Write to the appropriate agencies at the addresses provided in appendix B.

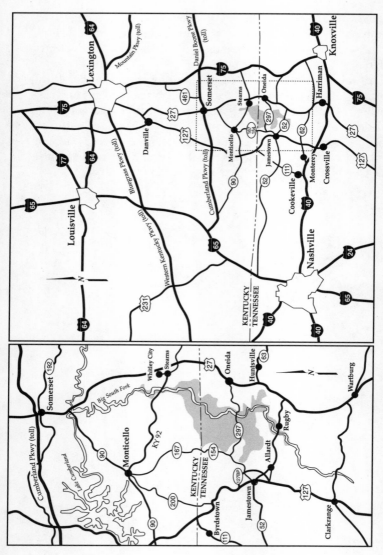

The Big South Fork National River and Recreation Area.

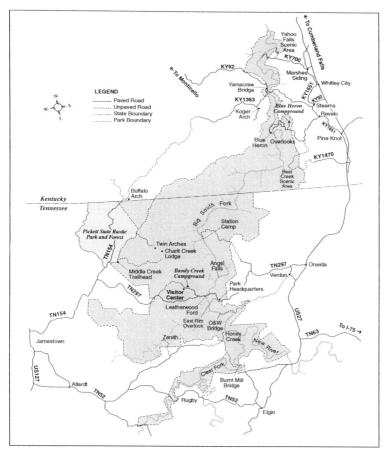

The Big South Fork Area.

SAFETY AND CONSERVATION

All the geological features in the area covered by this guidebook are fragile and vulnerable. They also are protected by law from improper activities. Please do not climb on any of these features or camp beneath them. You could injure yourself or destroy a part of our nation's natural heritage by climbing on, or disturbing, these geological resources. In addition, all archaeological and historical objects on public lands treated within this guide are protected by state and federal law from disturbance or theft. Report any vandalism of natural features or suspicious activity on the part of others to a park or forest ranger, or to some other law enforcement officer.

The Big South Fork area is a wonderful natural and recreational resource. But it is also a remote, wild area. As in all wilderness activities, you assume certain risks when you enter the backcountry. In addition to good camping skills, visitors to the backcountry of the Big South Fork area should have training, at a minimum, in basic first aid and should carry an adequate first-aid kit. Check with public health agencies such as the American Red Cross and/or hospitals and enroll in their first-aid and cardiopulmonary resuscitation (CPR) courses.

Two species of poisonous snakes exist in the area—the copperhead and the timber rattlesnake. These snakes inhabit the rocky areas and the forest floor of the Big South Fork area; the copperhead can be especially common. While poisonous snakebites are uncommon, they do occur here. Be observant when you walk or camp. Use a flashlight at night when walking, even on pavement, and wear shoes or boots. Poisonous snakes are cold-blooded reptiles. At night, when the ambient temperature may drop, the warmth of solar-heated pavement and gravel creates an environment favorable for snakes. Become familiar with first-aid treatments for snakebite by attending a first-aid or first-responder training course, as mentioned above.

Stinging insects such as yellow jackets, wasps, and hornets are common in spring, summer, and fall. Yellow jackets can be particularly bothersome, sometimes building their subterranean nests right on hiking trails. If you have a sensitivity to insect stings, be prepared. Check with your doctor about special medications for allergic reactions to insect bites, such as epinephrine applicators.

Ticks and chiggers are seasonally common, too. Ticks can carry lyme disease. Insect sprays can be helpful, although you should be sure to read the instructions before applying them to your skin. It is helpful to wear light-colored long pants so that ticks can be spotted and removed. You can also guard against ticks by tucking the legs of trousers into your boots. While hiking in tick country, it is advisable to stop periodically and check for ticks on your person. If you do find a tick attached to you, use tweezers and remove the insect by pulling it off. Be sure to remove the tick's head. Apply an antibiotic cream to the bite location for added protection. If redness or soreness persists in the bite area after removal, contact your medical doctor or other medical practitioner for advice.

Pay attention to weather forecasts and actual conditions before and during any backcountry excursion. Lightning can occur in any season, but summer afternoon storms can be especially dangerous. Seek shelter in safe areas during lightning storms. Stay away from exposed ridges or bluffs and solitary trees. Likewise, be careful near rivers and streams, especially if you plan to go boating. The best protection against stormy weather is to be prepared with knowledge of the local forecast.

Hunting is allowed on a seasonal basis in the Big South Fork National River and Recreation Area, Scott and Pickett state forests, and Daniel Boone National Forest. Become aware of hunting seasons and safety zones, and if you hike in hunting seasons, wear safety vests and safety hats or caps ("day-glo" orange in color). If you elect to visit the area during hunting seasons, stay on designated trails and make yourself visible. Information on hunting can be acquired from the National Park Service (NPS) visitor centers or from any park ranger or forest ranger in the Big South Fork area.

On any excursion, be sure to hike with a companion, wear boots with good tread, take along a compass and topo map, and let someone else know your itinerary and plans. The NPS has a backcountry registration form which you can complete at park visitor centers.

Boil or treat any water you get from streams, creeks, or springs. Do not drink any untreated water—serious illness or discomfort may occur.

Winter is a good time of year to look for natural arches. Poisonous snakes, chiggers, ticks, and stinging insects are all hibernating, and the vegetative cover is reduced. However, winter produces frost, ice, and snow which can make foot and vehicle travel hazardous. Be extremely careful of your footing while hiking in the winter. Be aware also that, at the drip line of cliffs, bluffs, rockshelters, and arches, large icicles can detach at any moment and come crashing down as sharp missiles. On any winter excursion, check the local weather forecast beforehand, and check on trail conditions and hunting activity with park rangers at visitor stations prior to entering the field. Be aware of the dangers of hypothermia (a dangerous lowering of the body's core temperature), and know how to prevent it. NPS visitor centers can provide information about this malady, and books on hiking contain helpful information.

Make sure that you have clothing appropriate for outdoor exploration, especially in the winter. Wool, fleece, pile, and Gore-Tex are excellent fabrics for wet and cold weather; avoid cotton garments in winter. Layer your clothing. Wear a wool or insulated hat. Insulated hunting or hiking boots with an aggressive tread are advisable. Take along extra-high-calorie food, as well as water. It is advisable to take an extra day's food with you, in case you have to spend the night out in the event of an emergency. Be extremely careful of frost, ice, and snow on trails and roads.

The areas around natural arches and rock shelters can contain potentially dangerous waterfalls, slippery cliffs, and bluffs. Stay away from cliffs and bluffs unless there is a safe and designated trail along these features.

The Big South Fork of the Cumberland is a wild river whose character can change dramatically, depending on rainfall. It has strong, swirling currents, undercut rocks, and submerged drop-offs and strainers. Swim, wade, and boat in the river at your own risk. If you intend to boat the river or its tributaries, check with park rangers at the visitor centers to ascertain river levels.

Please exercise caution on roads in this region. Many are winding and narrow gravel roads with two-way traffic. Be on the lookout for stray dogs and wildlife that might bound onto the roadway. If you don't have four-wheel drive, look at a road carefully. If it looks impassable for your street vehicle, park the car and walk in, or visit the area in the dry months. Most of the landforms featured in this guide are within a relatively short hiking distance from the road.

When leaving your vehicle at a trailhead, whether for a day hike or overnight backpacking, lock it and take valuables with you. Don't leave notes on the dashboard advertising your hiking plans, and don't leave copies of backcountry registration forms on view in your vehicle that might show your plans. Report any suspicious or criminal activity to the nearest park ranger or law enforcement officer.

In 1998, a severe winter snowstorm dumped over two feet of snow on the Big South Fork area, causing extensive "blowdown" (destruction) of trees. This event was followed by a tornado in May and several violent summer thunderstorms, causing further blowdown. As a consequence of this extreme weather, some of the trails to the arches in this guide were severely impacted. At the time of this writing, late in 1998, the trails in the BSFNRRA and Pickett State Park are open, but those in the Daniel Boone National Forest are still impaired. You may encounter blowdown and "dead-fall" (fallen timber) along some of the routes described in the national forest. The arches are still there; the going may be rougher in some places, however.

For a pleasant visit to this remarkable natural area, exercise personal caution and common safety sense in exploring any of the natural areas described in this book.

ACKNOWLEDGMENTS

I wish to thank several persons associated with government land management agencies for their assistance in interpreting the cultural history and geological features of the Appalachian Mountains and the Cumberland Plateau. Tom Des Jean, archaeologist with the National Park Service (NPS), read the section on the human use of the region and provided information and references on the fascinating archaeology and history of the Big South Fork area. Steve Bakaletz and Ron Cornelius of the NPS gave me an overview of the geology of the area. Thanks also to Steve Seven of the NPS.

I also wish to thank Park Ranger David Delk of Pickett State Park, who assisted me in locating and naming several arches in his park. Thanks also to Alan Wasik, park manager of Pickett Park, and to Billy Glen Smith and Jim Terry, former Pickett Park employees. Thanks also to Bill Brumm, Dan Crockett, and Edna Daugherty of the Daniel Boone National Forest.

Thanks to Conley Blevins and to John Burns, who has a passion for natural arches. Chuck Summers, an excellent photographer and consummate fan of the Big South Fork area, provided several outstanding images for use in this guide, as did David Morris and Kevin Kelley. Special acknowledgment is given to Ron Cornelius for translating my hand-drawn maps into professional computer-generated versions.

Hearty thanks go to Bob Wheeley, local river guide and Big South Fork explorer, who kindly showed me several geological features with which he was familiar.

Ronald Zurawski, director of the Tennessee Division of Geology, deserves thanks for suggesting several references on the geology of the Cumberland Plateau, and for extending permission to reproduce a drawing from his division's publications. The Tennessee Division of Geology has a surprising number of high-quality publications on the geology of the Cumberland Plateau and the adjacent Appalachian Mountains. Of special importance is the seminal work by James X. Corgan and John T. Parks, *The Natural Bridges of Tennessee*. This work is the fundamental reference for anyone interested in the natural arches of the Cumberland Plateau area.

I wish to extend sincere thanks to Dr. Jim Casada for his guidance in this project. Early on, Jennifer Siler, director of the University of Tennessee Press, told me that she had faith in my project; I am grateful for her unfailing encouragement.

INTRODUCTION

Nestled in the upland country of eastern Tennessee and southeastern Kentucky is a physiographical subprovince called the Northern Cumberland Plateau. Not merely an isolated geological region, it forms part of the larger Appalachian Plateaus Province, which extends south into Alabama and as far north as Pennsylvania.

In the middle of this Northern Cumberland Plateau are the wildlands of the Big South Fork, on the border between Tennessee and Kentucky. That's what the people of the area call it, simply "the Big South Fork," or "Big South Fork country." It is a plateau encompassing two hundred thousand or more acres of publicly owned upland forests, wild rivers, and sandstone gorges— land that today contains a Tennessee state park, two Tennessee state forests, a national forest, and a National Park Service unit. This is a canyon land, where brown turkey vultures soar and teeter effortlessly along the sandstone ridges on warm, shimmering updrafts from the gorge below.

Here, in summer twilight, the forest reverberates, as millions of katydids propel heavenward their seemingly endless mantras. This can also be a winter land of bare mixed-deciduous trees and green conifers, periodically swaddled in perfect white snow. It is a land of secretive animals, where barred and great horned owls prowl in deep darkness, announcing their existence late at night with lonely, plaintive hoots.

Most dramatically, though, this is a land of geological features: free-flowing mountain rivers and streams, naked sandstone bluffs, rockshelters, chimney rocks, and sandstone arches. Especially arches. Perhaps no area in the mountainous South has such a panoply of natural arches. The Big South Fork area even lays claim to the largest arch, the South Arch of Twin Arches. Of the paradoxically permanent and transient nature of the landscape, no better symbol can be found than the natural arches of the Big South Fork area.

However striking, natural arches are but one part of the surface geology of the plateau-and-canyon country of the Big South Fork. One day a number of years ago, the special topography of the region first began to register upon me. I was hiking alone on one of the trails in the river gorge, my head down watching the trail. I was preoccupied with such mundane things as usually occupy our minds—work, bills. Suddenly, as the trail turned left away from the gorge wall, I looked up. Above me, thousands of quartzite pebbles were embedded in the sandstone wall. I reached up and touched them. They looked and felt like the pebbles one finds along certain river banks. Apparently this was an ancestral pebble-and-sand bar that had been buried for millions of years and now formed part of the underlying strata of sandstone. I studied the scene.

These pebbles in the rock had been exposed by the Big South Fork River, as it carved out the gorge here. Probably these pebbles had been swept down some stream in a distant, misty time. Where the stream made a turn, the pebbles had been deposited as an alluvial fan on the outside bend. Or perhaps they were part of an ancient delta at the mouth of some verdant, subtropical river. In any case, most likely they had been part of an ancient waterway that had coursed through primordial Big South Fork country. Now they were part of its geological past.

I imagined what this very scene might have been like in that far-distant past. To be able to see and touch evidence of a geological event that occurred some 250 million years ago seemed significant. After touching that prehistoric river, now buried beneath hundreds of feet of other sedimentary rock, I realized that, in the Big South Fork country, the natural arches, chimney rocks, and even small things like pebbles in an ancient stream are powerfully important.

This guide is intended to introduce the general public to the fascinating geological features of the Big South Fork area. It is not a technical textbook on geology. Nor is it intended merely to help "arch hounds" add these features to their "life lists." Rather, this guide surveys the most impressive and accessible natural arches and geological features in the area, and describes the processes that created them. The area covered by this guide contains perhaps fifty or so arches (no one knows the exact total yet), along with several chimney rocks, the river gorge, and thousands of natural rockshelters. Many of these arches are small or inaccessible and have not even been named yet. Many are not located on trails or roads or unfortunately are on private property. A geological feature such as Double Arch, in the south end of the Big South Fork national area, with its unusual stacked arches, is indeed a very worthy feature. However, it is not readily accessible and is on "deferred property"—property which, as of this writing, has not been acquired by the National Park Service yet. Another interesting arch, Triangle Arch, in the Daniel Boone National Forest, is not readily accessible on a designated trail. These arches are excluded from this guide. This survey focuses on the most significant arches and features that are accessible to a visitor lacking specialized equipment and able to expend only a moderate amount of effort.

In some cases, the selection process was difficult. Various people would recommend arches which they thought should be included. I then would look for each arch by myself or in the company of the nominating individual. Many of these arches were inaccessible. These scouting missions were enjoyable, to be sure, and I was able to see some incredible country in the company of true arch fans. Bob Wheeley, a local whitewater guide and explorer who knows much about the Big South Fork backcountry, one day took me to Bob's Arch and Morning Arch, two outstanding features. Morning Arch has the greatest width of any arch that I have seen in the Big South Fork, and Bob's Arch is a "window" opening in a finger ridge. However, these arches are not near trails. Getting to them required off-trail hiking with no definable benchmark.

On one occasion, National Park Service archaeologist Tom Des Jean invited me to accompany him and John Burns, another arch aficionado, to see an arch called "Nee High," on the Tennessee side of the Big South Fork national area. We hiked three miles along the John Muir Trail and then descended cross-country into a side canyon below the bluff, pushing back rhododendrons and briars as we progressed slowly through copperhead country. This was in late June, and the temperature was 90° F. There was no trail down to the arch. When we arrived, we crawled into the back of a dark rockshelter. Crouching in semidarkness, we looked out at the arch deck spanning the entrance. The arch span consisted of a cantilevered, sagging window deck about twenty feet long, running from wall to wall at eye level in the front of the alcove. The arch lintel had a crack through it where cantilevered segments joined. We took low-light photos and admired the scene. On the way out, we enjoyed a nearby waterfall (called "Joy" Falls) cascading down rhododendron-lined bluffs. The climb back out was just as interesting as the descent. Even though this is a splendid arch feature, it is inaccessible to the general public.

I selected the geological features discussed in this guide based on several criteria. The feature had to be (1) reasonably accessible by the general visitor in a regular street vehicle (i.e., a vehicle lacking four-wheel drive and high clearance); (2) significant (in terms of size, shape, or other feature) or a good representative of one of the several origin processes for natural features; (3) within approximately a mile and a half of a public access point near a road or trail; (4) on public land.

Although it excludes some arches which do not meet the criteria, this guide nevertheless identifies most of the known significant geological features in Pickett State Park, the Big South Fork National River and Recreation Area, and the Daniel Boone National Forest (Stearns District). The guide treats twenty-six destinations; many of these contain multiple geological features or processes. For example, the trail to Cracks-in-the-Rock passes by a grotto of dwarf column arches in an area five feet wide; Hazard Cave displays both a rockshelter and a window arch; and New, Yahoo, and Markers arches each encompass smaller window arches. These features are illustrative of the major geological processes that have shaped—and continue to shape—the Big South Fork country.

Even though one criterion for inclusion in this guide is general accessibility, few of the geological features described here can be reached merely by driving up to them in a motor vehicle. A moderate amount of off-pavement travel usually is required, followed in many cases (as at Buffalo Arch and Gobbler's Arch) by a short hike. This is as it should be with any natural wonder; a important feature should be seen in its natural setting.

Using this guide, the visitor will pass through some pretty impressive hiking terrain. The Big South Fork area contains some of the roughest and most beautiful backcountry in the eastern United States. The area offers great opportunities for mountain biking, horseback riding, canoeing, kayaking, rafting, hiking, and backpacking. Most of the arches and features in this guide are located on or near trails that lead to other significant recreational, cultural, and natural attractions.

This Big South Fork country exerts its appeal in a subtle manner. It doesn't blow you away with panoramic mountain vistas like the Great Smokies or, say, the Tetons. There are plenty of vistas here; it is just that you don't see them coming from miles away. The Big South Fork is plateau country; you are either on the plateau or below it. Therefore, the views are horizontal or even downhill, as with the river gorge and all its side canyons. Here you really have to want to see things and get there.

I remember my first trip to the area and my first view of Twin Arches. It was in October 1978, twenty years ago. In those days, the Big South Fork did not have much of what we today call "infrastructure." This was only four years after Congress first authorized the Big South Fork National River and Recreation Area. It was tough getting around on the four-wheel-drive Jeep roads; you had to hope that, if you could get in, you also could get out.

I was with a Sierra Club outing into the area, and I honestly didn't know where I was when we got to Twin Arches. I couldn't have remembered how to get back in there if you'd asked me later. We were staying at Pickett State Park nearby, and someone had mentioned a day trip to see these features. I agreed to go along.

In those days, there were no blazed hiking trails and no wooden stairs to aid us in getting down to the arches, as there are today. To me the area was strange and mysterious. Upon arrival at the Twin Arches, our group dispersed, with everyone wandering around on his or her own for a time. I somehow found myself on the top of the South Arch, which looks more like a ridgeline than an arch span. I did not know at the time that I was out on the arch deck; I thought I was merely out on a finger ridge. Arriving at the end of the ridge, I stopped. From this perch the whole earth seemed to open up, as the south span dipped down like a shoulder toward the valley of Station Camp Creek. I remember a distinct feeling of vertigo. I eased back, recovered, and soon settled into the scene.

It was one of those warm October Saturdays that you wish would last forever. The view spread out over Station Camp Creek's drainage area, with Charit Creek just to the east. A seemingly endless forest, bisected only by a tawny line of cliffs in the green distance, lay before me. I sat down and relaxed.

That day twenty years ago was my first experience with the lonely and magical landscape of the Big South Fork country. As I

Aerial View of Twin Arches Finger Ridge. Courtesy of National Park Service, U.S. Department of the Interior.

sat contemplating the view, the wind blew steadily, singing through the Virginia pines on top of the arch. Perhaps the wind sang, too, as it coursed through the arch opening below me, like some large flute. Perhaps the breeze really does sing, inaudible to us, through these earth woodwinds.

My image of that day long ago, when I was a younger man with no gray in my beard, is like an old Polaroid snapshot, dulled and yellowed at the corners but full of warm memories. After that day, I returned often to the Big South Fork country, mainly to hike and to paddle its streams. For the past five years, I have lived in the gorge country. Even so, I still sense a certain enigmatic nature about the landscape. I hope I never lose that feeling. Like most outdoorspeople, I certainly want to know the science of a natural area, but I also want to retain some sense of its enduring mystery. Today, even with all the guidebooks and maps and improvements in access to the area, the Big South Fork country still seems somewhat mysterious to me.

The arches and features described herein are the best of the best. After visiting them, you should be able to appreciate more fully the forces that have shaped the surface geology of the region. This guide includes representative examples of the various types of natural arches and geological features found in the Big South Fork country, from arches created by such processes as "headward erosion" and "widening of a joint," to unique features with bizarre shapes, such as chimney rocks. These geological features are indeed the signature pieces of the Big South Fork region, perhaps even more characteristic of the area than the Big South Fork River itself, that master sculptor of the geological scene. They set this area apart from the rest of the southern highlands.

There are other wild gorges in the eastern uplands of North America, but only the Big South Fork area offers such a dynamic array of truly significant natural sculptures within a generally accessible area. Explore them with a sense of mystery and wonder. Enjoy.

Part 1
The Resources

THE LAND

The Big South Fork country is located in a geological subprovince called the Northern Cumberland Plateau, a part of the larger Cumberland Plateau, which is part of the still larger Appalachian Plateaus Province. The Northern Cumberland Plateau is bounded on the south by the Sequatchie Valley, on the east by the Valley and Ridge Province, and on the west by the Eastern Highland Rim (Luther 1959, 31, 34; Luther 1977, vii). The subprovince continues northward into McCreary County, Kentucky. The exposed rock of the Northern Cumberland Plateau is sedimentary.

Looking at the overall topography of the Big South Fork country, one sees a generally flat, wooded plateau, extending to cliff faces of the stream canyons. The top of the plateau is characterized by broad, upland ridges, narrow finger ridges, and cliff lines. Below the cliffs, there are steep-sided slopes, benched slopes, gradual colluvial slopes, and narrow stream terraces above river level. The caprock of the Big South Fork area is predominantly Rockcastle Conglomerate sandstone, a Pennsylvanian Period sedimentary rock. The sandstone is clastic, which means it is made up of fragmented grains of sand, silts, or other rocks. It is a medium- to coarse-grained conglomerate, with quartzite pebbles often visible. The sandstone is around 250 million years old. Rockcastle Conglomerate is widely dispersed on the northern plateau (Luther 1959, 16).

Descending from the bluff of the plateau, down the cliffs or ledges, and into the V-shaped valley of the Big South Fork of the Cumberland River and its tributaries, one encounters *rockshelters.* These are rock awnings or overhangs of sandstone where less resistant rock below eroded or weathered away, leaving the harder sandstone above to form an alcove. The erosion of the softer sandstone beneath these overhangs can cause rock debris to roll down the V-shaped slopes of the gorge toward the river and side creeks. This rock debris forms a colluvial block collection on the talus slopes and in the floodplain of the streams.

Mixed within and below the capstone Rockcastle Conglomerate are beds of shale, which also can contain seams of coal (Luther

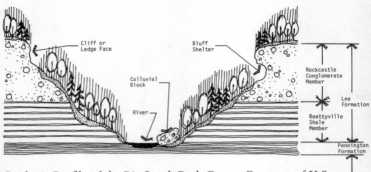

Geologic Profile of the Big South Fork Gorge. Courtesy of U.S. Army Corps of Engineers.

1959, 12; Luther 1977, 58). Coal was mined extensively in the area from the beginning of this century until recently.

The Cumberland Plateau landscape offers not high peaks but varied landforms eked out of the prevailing sandstone caprock that dates from the Pennsylvanian Period. This rock was formed by sedimentary deposits from river channels, lakes, and shallow inland seas some 250 million years ago, when the climate of the area most likely was tropical. Most of the Big South Fork country is Pennsylvanian age rock, rock of the Paleozoic Era; only a small amount of older upper Mississippian limestone is exposed in the northern sections of the area (Gaydos 1982, 8; Byrne et al. 1964, 78).

The Big South Fork area can be compared (albeit on a smaller scale) to the Colorado Plateau country of the American West, with its Grand Canyon, Bryce Canyon, Zion, and Canyonlands. Big South Fork, however, has trees—lots of trees—and other vegetation. I like to play a little mind game when I'm looking at the topography here. Gazing out at the plateau and gorges, I mentally strip away the vegetation and try to visualize the remaining rocky scene, as if I were in Arizona or Utah, looking at a desert canyon. I remember reading some geologist's lament that, in the East, you couldn't "see the geology for the trees." It might seem exaggerated, but there's something to that statement. In the West, the geology literally jumps out at you. There, with a little effort, you can see, right in front of you, the river gorges, side canyons, natural arches, fault lines, synclines and anticlines, old volcano cones and lava flows. In the eastern United States, all those trees and the other vegetation get in the way. In the East, you have to be resourceful. By using a little imagination and by looking at areas where the vegetation has been removed, however, one can see the prevailing external sedimentary geology. The East does have one advantage—roadcuts. With the extensive road system here, highway roadcuts offer portals into eastern geology. Roadcuts may be the single biggest boon to the interpretation of surface geology in this section of the country.

The dominant story at Big South Fork, as at Grand Canyon and Bryce Canyon, is water erosion and weathering. Here, water is cutting down through sedimentary rock, wending its way inexorably to the sea. This region contains no geological "hot spots," nor any volcanism, at least not in the present geological age. Consequently, no igneous or even metamorphic rock lies exposed in the Big South Fork country. Uplift and movement have occurred in and around the Cumberland Plateau in the geological past, however. A great example can be seen on the eastern edge of the plateau, just off Interstate Highway 75 on the north edge of Cove Lake State Park, about forty miles north of Knoxville, Tennessee. Here, the observant motorist can view an awesome scene of formerly horizontal sedimentary strata thrusting vertically upward. Where erosion and weathering have created a knife-edge aspect, large vertical slabs of rock protrude west out of the dominant ridge. These rocks—referred to variously by local folks and rock climbers as the "Devil's Racetrack" or the Caryville Rocks—show us that dramatic geological forces did clash on the edge of the plateau in the distant geological past.

Through the ages, erosion and weathering have continued to shape the landscape in the Big South Fork area. Sandstone laid down by ancient seas and lakes in the Pennsylvanian Period has been eroded over thousands of years to form the unique features visible today. The area contains many significant geological features. Principal among these are the natural arches, also called natural bridges. They are indeed the signature pieces of the Big South Fork country.

Formation of Arches

The natural arches of the Big South Fork area are by-products of past sedimentation and erosion. Here you have an uplifted sandstone plateau, where erosion has carved out a major system of gorges and clifflines, creating a large water drainage off the Cumberland Plateau. In the Big South Fork country, you generally find arches on the edges of gorge bluffs or on ridges near the blufflines. This is not surprising, because arches are formed as water moves down, across, and through horizontal sandstone ridges toward the gorge of the Big South Fork of the Cumberland River.

Arches come in all shapes and sizes. There are natural arches—that is, any hole through a sedimentary ridge, mountain, or rock (for example, Second Chance Arch in Pickett Civilian Conservation Corps Memorial State Park). Then there are natural bridges—features exhibiting the shape and symmetry of bridge spans (for example, Natural Arch in the Daniel Boone National Forest). This variety makes these natural rock features all the more appealing.

Specialized terms designate the special components of arches. When you look at a natural arch or natural bridge, you see a span of rock forming the bridge or roof of the arch. This bridge is called the *lintel*. The flat plankway or surface that often appears on the top of the lintel is called the *deck*. The *span* is the amount of horizontal open space beneath the arch or bridge (the measurable space between the arch *pillars*, or side supports). Sometimes the span is also referred to as *width*. The *clearance* of an arch is the maximum height beneath the bridge or arch, the vertical distance from the floor beneath the bridge to the lintel (Corgan and Parks 1979, 3–4). Clearance often is referred to as the *height* of an arch.

Many measurements in the literature on local arches specify height and width rather than span and clearance. For simplicity's sake, in this guidebook, unless otherwise noted, I have adopted this popular practice.

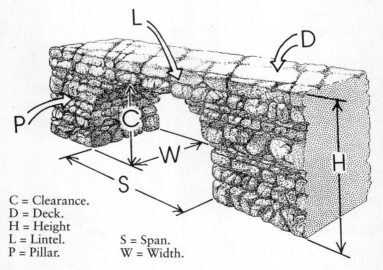

C = Clearance.
D = Deck.
H = Height
L = Lintel.
P = Pillar.   S = Span.
                     W = Width.

Descriptive Terms for Natural Arches and Bridges. Courtesy of Tennessee Division of Geology.

Just as an engineer has to calculate and provide for the handling of stresses in buildings and bridge spans, so does nature have to provide support for natural arches. In any natural arch, natural bridge, or cave, there is a *tension dome* (Corgan and Parks 1979, 9, 11). Since there is no rock support below the lintel of an arch, the task of supporting the structure is distributed throughout the freestanding span of rock. This distribution of stress creates a tension dome in which a rock stratum (or strata) in the lintel acts like a structural beam, bearing the weight of the arch. Through erosion and time, these support strata can sag and eventually collapse, either enlarging the span or destroying the feature.

Natural arches develop by several processes. These are examined below.

Widening of a Joint

Seeping water and waterfalls descending from the bluffs can widen joints or cracks in the sandstone behind the lip of waterfalls or in between rock blocks. This water percolates down and through the bluff, gradually eroding and separating a span of sandstone from the main bluffline and ultimately creating freestanding arch spans (Corgan and Parks 1979, 13, 15).

Headward Erosion

Arches also can be formed by "headward erosion." Here, water falling off the bluff creates an active gully which expands up a slope, sometimes on both sides of a ridge. Ultimately the water cuts through less resistant sandstone beneath the surface and opens a hole through the ridge. This hole initially is very small (sometimes it is referred to as a *lighthouse* in a cliff). Headward erosion by water falling from above continues to expand up the slope, creating a hole in the bluff or tying in with a lighthouse hole. Headward erosion usually creates arches which are large and symmetrical (Corgan and Parks 1979, 9).

Collapse of Rockshelters

Arches also can be formed by the collapse of rockhouses or rockshelters, those rock overhangs below the bluffs and ridges in the Big South Fork country. These rockshelters are like large cave entrances. When water percolates downward through cracks in the sandstone comprising the rockshelters, it sometimes encounters shale or coal beds. These beds can divert the water horizontally, and weaker sandstone can be compromised and a collapse may occur. The collapse may bring down the entire rockshelter, or it may leave part of the roof. In this latter case, part of the roof of the former rockshelter now forms a span or lintel which is separated from the host ridge behind, creating an arch.

You usually can detect which arches have been caused in this fashion by the amount of sandstone breakdown beneath the lintel. A large amount of breakdown usually exists beneath these arches, testifying to their violent and catastrophic origin, in contrast to the sandy floors of arches caused by headward erosion. Arches caused by collapse also usually have sharp angles and a more ragged overall appearance; they lack the smooth and graceful symmetry of arches formed more gradually.

In other areas of Tennessee and Kentucky, collapse of limestone caves also can create natural arches or bridges (Corgan and Parks 1979, 5–8).

Gravity

Gravity, too, can shape natural arches. Arches created by gravity collapse are described as being the product of catastrophic events and usually are not as symmetrical as those caused by slow and meticulous headward erosion. The category of gravity-formed arches contains three groups: arches formed by *rockfall,* by *creep,* and by *sagging* (Corgan and Parks 1979, 12).

Rockfall arches occur when a rock falls down over a rock depression, spanning the depression and forming a sort of prefabricated arch (an example is Devil's Arch in the Big South Fork area to the west of Blue Heron).

Creep arches occur on steep terrain, where the pull of gravity causes rocks to slowly "creep" downhill over other rocks, sometimes forming a roof. This process differs from the more rapid and catastrophic episodes of movement resulting in rockfall arches. Both rockfall and creep arches usually are asymmetrical (Corgan and Parks 1979, 12).

Sagging occurs when rocks that form the tension dome over the mouth of a rockshelter sag as they are exposed to differential erosion, causing a thin span to become separated—stretched, as it were—across the roof entrance. This is a unique geological process (Corgan and Parks 1979, 12). Hazard Cave Window Arch (see description in this guide) in Pickett State Park in the Big South Fork area is a very interesting example of this process.

Incised Meanders

This is a unique arch phenomenon. A deeply cut stream meanders around a weakly formed narrow finger ridge. Over long periods of time, the persistent force of the meandering stream pierces through the weak neck section of the rock ridgeline on one side.

Concurrently, the stream continues eroding out the ridgeline on the opposite meander side, eventually opening up a hole. The stream then can pass through the narrow ridge to join itself on the opposite side, continuing to enlarge the hole at high water levels. This is a rare and fascinating method of arch construction, and area visitors can examine it at Pickett Lake Natural Bridge in Pickett State Park (Corgan and Parks 1979, 16).

Cave Collapse

In limestone karst areas, cave sinkholes may collapse due to fatigue caused by erosion. The collapse sometimes opens up a clearance through a hill or ridge (Corgan and Parks 1979, 5–8). Since the Big South Fork area's external features are predominantly sandstone and not limestone, this process is not seen. There are some limestone caves north of the Big South Fork area, in Wayne and Somerset counties in Kentucky, but these lie outside the geographical scope of this guidebook.

All the above processes can work independently or in collaboration to yield natural bridges or arches. In the Big South Fork area, arches are formed because the sandstone here is not uniform. Some is hard and resistant, and some is soft and crumbly. In the same general locale, you can find sandstone which will crumble under hand pressure and some which feels like iron.

Because there is such a difference in the texture of the area's sandstone, not all the rocks in the Big South Fork area erode at the same rate of speed. When certain rock strata in the same climate are more resistant to weathering and erosion than others, geologists call this *differential erosion* (Harris and Tuttle 1990, 26). Differential erosion is widespread in the Big South Fork country. You can find examples in the many honeycomb holes beneath certain arches and rockshelters, and in the formation of chimney rocks.

The Formation of Chimney Rocks

Chimney rocks are resistant spires of hard sandstone which refused to erode. You can see imposing chimney spires in the sandstone canyon country of Utah and Arizona, at Arches National Park and in Monument Valley. If you've watched John Wayne's western movies filmed in Monument Valley, you've probably noticed chimney spires in the background. Here in the Big South Fork, the chimney rocks are smaller, but they reflect the same formation process.

When you look at the chimney rocks here, you see irregular columns with capstones on their summits. The tops of the columns show where the prevailing sandstone layer was located prior to the erosion which wore away the softer surrounding rock. In many cases, the resistant caps on these spires protected the sandstone below from erosion, yielding the pedestal formation. These chimneys demonstrate just how much erosion has occurred in an area. By being resistant to erosion, they have created another unique geological feature, one that is rare in the eastern United States. The largest chimney rock I have seen in the Big South Fork area (located northeast of the Terry Cemetery and south of No Business Creek) was shown to me by Bob Wheeley, a local river runner and explorer. This chimney, called Cap Rock, is approximately fifty feet in height, with a window hole in it. It is a major sedimentary feature in the area. Unfortunately, this chimney rock is not located near an accessible, designated trail. However, two significant and very accessible chimney rocks are located conveniently along Station Camp Road. These are described in this guidebook.

The Formation of Rockshelters

Rockshelters are the commonest notable geological feature in the Big South Fork country. Thousands of them are dispersed throughout the region. Rockshelters, also called rockhouses, are natural alcoves beneath the sandstone cliffs of the Cumberland Plateau. Both the common names suggest a domicile of sorts, which is a cultural description, not a geological one. Historically, and prehistorically, humans have used these overhangs for shelter, even as visitors looking for natural arches might use them today for temporary shelter on a rainy day.

As far back as ten thousand years ago, prehistoric Indians used the rockshelters of the Big South Fork country extensively (National Park Service Wayside Exhibit, Yahoo Falls, Big South Fork). Visit Hazard Cave or Yahoo Falls, and you'll see why. These natural "houses" provided roaming bands of aboriginal hunters and gatherers with dry places out of the elements. Most of these rockshelters have some seasonal water nearby, so they made convenient abodes for Native Americans in the distant past.

White settlers also took advantage of the temporary shelter these places afford. The first "long hunters" who ventured into the Big South Fork area in the 1770s undoubtedly took up temporary lodging beneath these overhangs. Some pioneer farmers even fenced in the open side and kept pigs and cattle in a natural pen or corral (Department of the Interior, National Park Service, Big South Fork National River and Recreation Area, *A Guide to the Oscar Blevins Loop Trail*).

Rockshelters are formed through the erosion of softer layers of sandstone below a bluff or cliff. The principle is the same as in the formation of arches: water seeps over and through blufflines, waterfalls, and cracks and erodes the softer sandstone below the lip of the bluff, creating an alcove. In fact, some of the natural arches described in this guidebook were once rockshelters in which the back eroded away or caved in, leaving the front to form the lintel and deck of an arch. Koger Arch (described in this book) is a good example. Rockshelters, found throughout the backcountry of the Big South Fork, exemplify the important role erosion has played in the surface geology of the area.

Erosion shaped the natural arches, rockshelters, and chimney rocks that we see today, as indeed it continues to shape our local landscape. Eventually all the current arches and other features will fall down from their own weight. It is inevitable. But other arches and chimney rocks are slowly being formed elsewhere in the area to take their place. The cycle will continue.

This is the geological scene we behold. From the ancient sedimentary rocks laid down over two hundred million years ago, to the extensive erosion occurring up to the present, this landscape is a changing canvas upon which nature paints her works of art. The Big South Fork of the Cumberland River, the complex gorge and side canyon system, the natural arches, rockshelters, and chimney rocks are truly the geological heritage of the Big South Fork area.

THE RIVER

The Big South Fork region is named after the major river which has shaped it, the Big South Fork of the Cumberland River. This river has several major tributaries which also have helped to shape the land. The initial sculptors of this natural gallery are the New and Clear Fork rivers in Tennessee, which join to form the Big South Fork. Other tributaries also join in farther downstream; some are Pine Creek, North White Oak Creek, Bandy Creek, Station Camp Creek, Parch Corn Creek, No Business Creek, Bear Creek, and Rock Creek. But the New and Clear Fork rivers are the headwater progenitors of the Big South Fork of the Cumberland River.

New River (not to be confused with the larger New River Gorge in West Virginia) begins in the mountains of northwestern Anderson County, Tennessee. It drains a watershed area of 396 square miles. In its headwaters it is steep and swift, with an average drop of 125 feet per mile (U.S. Army Corps of Engineers et al. 1969, 26). The New calms down as drop-per-mile decreases in the next 30 miles; it terminates after 55 miles, as it joins Clear Fork River in Scott County, Tennessee (ibid., 24; U.S. Army Corps of Engineers, "Big South Fork Master Plan," vol. 1:4–4).

Clear Fork, whose headwaters are in southeastern Fentress County, Tennessee, is a true mountain stream; there is no large bottomland floodplain in all its 40-mile length. It drains a watershed of some 283 square miles (U.S. Army Corps of Engineers et al. 1969, 24). It receives a seasonally significant contribution from White Oak Creek, which flows north out of Morgan County and joins Clear Fork east of the town of Rugby, Tennessee. Clear Fork then flows purposefully under Burnt Mill Bridge, heading north and gaining speed as it approaches its termination as a named stream at its canyon junction with New River. This junction is known to Big South Fork river runners as "the confluence."

In their nascent stirrings, the New and Clear Fork rivers writhe generally northward, cutting moderate ravines and forming a Y as they descend down and through the Northern Cumberland Plateau. They coalesce in the rocky and remote depths of a sandstone canyon, forming at their convergence a bigger mountain river, the Big South Fork.

The Big South Fork muscles and grinds its way through the red heart of this terrain. Master of the country, it is an entrenched river, confined within a sandstone canyon. In its 77-mile length, it drops a total of 413 feet (U.S. Army Corps of Engineers et al. 1969, 24). Like a seasoned sculptor, this river is patient and persistent. After all, it has been at its work for millions of years. The river can be quiet at times; at other times, during and after rainstorms, it can become angry as tens of thousands of cubic feet of runoff from the plateau bluffs fall 400 feet into the narrow gorge. Water is the agent of change in this country.

The Big South Fork of the Cumberland differs from, say, the Tennessee River, or the Holston, or the Clinch, which are some other nearby streams. For one thing, it flows north—for its entire length. The elevation and geology of the Cumberland Plateau caused the ancestral Big South Fork runoff to flow north, the direction of least resistance. Grinding its way through the stone of least resistance, sandstone, the river bent and turned. After a journey of more than a hundred miles (counting its headwater tributaries), it joins the main Cumberland River in southeastern Kentucky. Then it finally flows west-southwest, like the majority of contemporary trans-Appalachian streams, toward the great midcontinental drainages of the Ohio and Mississippi rivers. For

Confluence of New and Clear Fork Rivers. Courtesy of National Park Service, U.S. Department of the Interior.

some one hundred miles, though, the Big South Fork of the Cumberland is truly unique.

The Big South Fork is also a natural river. No dams hamper the flow of this waterway or any of its tributaries. For an eastern river so close to the Tennessee Valley Authority (TVA) and the U.S. Army Corps of Engineers, this is a great distinction. In fact, the United States Senate authorized a dam for Big South Fork in the 1930s, and for years it appeared that funding someday would come through and the dam would be built (Baker and Netherton 1993, 23). The Army Corps of Engineers came in and started making plans. Fortunately, for over thirty years the House of Representatives declined to join the Senate in endorsing the dam (25). In the early 1970s, it was decided that no dam would ever be built on the Big South Fork. Seeing the handwriting on the wall, the Corps of Engineers became a partner in establishing a National Park Service unit instead.

With the demise of plans for a dam came a respite from resource degradation. For some sixty years, coal mining and timber operations along the river and its tributaries had poured millions of tons of siltation and mine spoils into the river, destroying its clarity and its chemistry. The river needed a breather. When the area became a national park unit, open-slope mines were sealed or reclaimed, and monitoring of water quality began. The aquatic health of the river is improving, although threats from outside the boundaries of the federal preserve still exist.

Today the river is a popular sport fishery for bass, bluegill, walleye, sauger, muskellunge, and catfish. The river also is a regionally significant whitewater recreational magnet, its undammed waters attracting thousands of rafters, kayakers, and canoeists. Those seeking whitewater thrills particularly relish the challenging "gorge and canyon" section of the river, from Burnt Mill Bridge on the Clear Fork River downstream to Leatherwood Ford on the main river, a float of 11 miles. When the water is up, it is a dynamic run. Take a raft trip down this stretch of canyon whitewater with a professional river outfitter. The whitewater will keep you busy, with such named rapids as Double Falls, the Washing Machine, and the Ell coming at you fast. But now and then you'll get a rock-level view of the geology of the area before Rion's Eddy, Jake's Hole, and O&W Rapid reclaim your attention. All too soon (if you like whitewater), you'll take out at Leatherwood Ford after your Cumberland Plateau wilderness float.

Downstream from Leatherwood Ford, the river drop decreases and the river slows as it snakes northward to Kentucky. The big whitewater is upstream, but several challenging rapids remain in the next 28 miles, like Angel Falls and Devil's Jump (these should be portaged).

You don't have to be a fisherman or kayaker to feel the essence of the river system, although those are admirable ways of getting to know the river. Several overlooks provide vistas into the river life of this region. Hike out to the Honey Creek Overlook for a view of the river canyon. To get to Honey Creek, take U.S. Highway 27 south from Oneida, Tennessee, for 11 miles. You'll see a brown and white National Park Service sign on the right, reading "Burnt Mill Bridge River Access 4-1/2 miles." Follow the signs thereafter to Burnt Mill Bridge, cross the bridge, and proceed approximately 3.5 miles to the parking area for the Honey Creek Overlook. A short trail leads to the overlook. It not only affords a great view, but the hike provides a wonderful exposure to the backcountry of the Big South Fork.

Or, for a view of the main river, hike from Leatherwood Ford up the John Muir Trail to Angel Falls Overlook. This 3-mile (one way) hike takes you from the riparian world of the river at Leatherwood Ford up to the crest of the Cumberland Plateau for an amazing view of the river canyon and the adjacent plateau country.

Several developed overlooks can be reached by very short strolls from your motor vehicle. In Tennessee, the East Rim Overlook off Tennessee Highway 297 is readily accessible from a paved parking lot, as are the Devil's Jump and Gorge Overlooks in Kentucky.

Running the Washing Machine, Big South Fork River Gorge. Courtesy of National Park Service, U.S. Department of the Interior.

The best view in the park, however, is the Bear Creek Overlook, which requires hiking only a level 0.3 mile one way (the directions to this overlook are given in this guidebook, in the description of Split Bow Arch). The view from Bear Creek Overlook, particularly at sunset, is spectacular. You look upstream at the river as it flows toward you through what appears to be total wilderness. Below, the river bends to the left where Bear Creek converges with it. Off to the west, the forests of the Big South Fork park and the Daniel Boone National Forest roll on and on into the setting sun. This incredible view contains no obvious signs of human impact.

Be sure to check out these views of the river system. The overlooks and directions to them are given in the park brochure for the Big South Fork National River and Recreation Area. It is available free from the National Park Service.

As a natural river, the Big South Fork of the Cumberland is not the same every day. Its life is symbiotic with that of the sky. When there is rain, the river growls and churns. When the weather is dry, the river is slender and demure. On dry, hot summer days, it can resemble a slow creek, with many places so shallow you can wade across on horseback or foot. River flow in late summer can register as low as 50 cubic feet per second (cfs) on the river-level gauge. That's about the size of a somnolent creek. Come the rainy season (winter and spring), however, hang onto your hat. During this time, the river can equal the Colorado in the Grand Canyon, with readings of 20,000 to 30,000 cfs or more. And it doesn't take long for the river to surge. Extreme water levels can develop with only twelve to twenty-four hours of steady rain, and such rains are not uncommon. Every year the river attains high levels several times, as the huge plateau drainage quickly propels its load downstream toward the sea. At these times, the river is mean, dirty, and angry, muscling and grinding its way through its mountain canyon. It is then you can see its geological power. Few places in the southeastern mountains allow us to see the spectacle of a free river in all its raw power.

We can be thankful that no dams were ever built in this drainage. Today the free and unconquered river still courses through the Big South Fork country. As it has done for millions of years past, the river is shaping the land around it for a thousand years to come. Its passage through this fascinating geologic area can best be summed up by paraphrasing a succinct quotation from a Sierra Club book of thirty years ago about the Grand Canyon: "The Big South Fork—Time and the River Flowing."

THE AREA AND HUMANS

The Big South Fork area lies on the Northern Cumberland Plateau, straddling the boundary between East Tennessee and southeastern Kentucky. The region covered by this guidebook includes parts of Scott, Pickett, and Fentress counties in Tennessee, and McCreary County in Kentucky. Our study region is the area in and around the Big South Fork National River and Recreation Area (BSFNRRA), Scott State Forest, Pickett State Park and Forest, and the Stearns and Somerset districts of the Daniel Boone National Forest.

For years, the Big South Fork area was viewed as an exploitable resource; its timber and mineral resources were very valuable. From the beginning of this century through the 1960s, the park area's resources were exploited (Manning 1994, 100–108).

Always a relatively remote area, the Big South Fork region in Civil War days was labeled on maps simply "The Wilderness" (Baker and Netherton 1993, 19). The gorge and side canyons of the Big South Fork of the Cumberland River, the dense stands of mixed hardwoods and conifers, and the impenetrable laurel thickets in the drainages—these made travel and commerce tenuous at best. The human population never has been large, as farming generally has been marginal and jobs few. The lack of good transportation corridors contributed to the economic isolation. The forest did allow for subsistence hunting to supplement the marginal agriculture.

Place names on the map give us an idea of what the first white settlers faced. One area on the Tennessee side of the Big South Fork is called "No Business." Tradition has it that the wife of one of the settlers in the valley said they had no business being in such a place. The name also described the lack of economic activity in the isolated valley. Local folks also called a creek in the area "Difficulty," perhaps describing their lives in general. And they pronounced it "dif-*fick*-ul-ty." Two other creeks not far away are named "Lonesome" and "Troublesome."

We know that European Americans were not the first humans to traverse this land. Abundant prehistoric evidence proves that ancient bands of humans found something in this plateau and canyon country to justify their staying awhile. Thousands of archaeological sites are estimated to be located in the Big South Fork area (Baker and Netherton 1993, 18; Des Jean 1998, personal communication). Some impulsive past commentators labeled this area "the Mesa Verde of the East," in a rather incongruous reference to a much different culture of Anasazi cliff-dwellers and basket makers in distant Colorado.

Archaeologists, being a somewhat more cautious lot, concede that the area is rich in several prehistoric cultural traditions, most far earlier in origin than the Anasazi of the Southwest. In fact, evidence of the earliest cultural tradition of the southeastern United States, that of the *Paleo-Indian,* has been found in the Big South Fork region. According to National Park Service archaeologist Tom Des Jean, six Paleo-Indian projectile points have been found within the boundary of the BSFNRRA (Des Jean 1998, personal communication). Early and Late Paleo-Indian materials also have been discovered in Great Rock Sink in Pulaski County, Kentucky, just north of the BSFNRRA (Des Jean and Benthall 1994, 95). While not extensive, the evidence suggests that Paleo-Indians may have used the Big South Fork country in a limited fashion as far back as ten to twelve thousand years ago. (117).

For millions of years, human sounds, activities, and impacts were absent from what would later become the United States. While Africa, Asia, and Europe experienced human occupation thousands of years earlier, the misty uplands of Tennessee and Kentucky were devoid of human sounds (Hudson 1976, 36). Then, perhaps fifteen thousand years ago, the first human feet trod upon North American soil (ibid., 37; Lewis and Kneberg 1958, 3). Many archaeologists believe that Ice Age hunters from Asia crossed a land mass known as the Bering Strait Land Bridge (now submerged beneath the Bering Sea) and entered what we call Alaska. They accomplished this journey during ice ages, when the level of oceans was lower, worldwide, due to the fact that so much water was locked up in ice. These low-water periods exposed land bridges, hundreds of miles wide, which previously had been submerged (Hudson 1976, 37). During the last ice age, a land bridge between Asia and North America may have been exposed several times, providing a route for humans (37–38). There is strong evidence that the first migration of humans into the New World occurred from Siberia during glacial periods in the Pleistocene Ice Age (36). This migration by Asian aboriginal people following game animals was a momentous event in the cultural and natural history of this continent.

If Asian nomads did cross the Bering land bridge to North

America, then their descendants may have migrated into what we know today as the lower forty-eight states (Hudson 1976, 36–37). Obviously, the first Ice Age hunters who set foot in Alaska were not the humans who made it to the Big South Fork country. Could they have been the ancestors of aboriginal peoples who populated Kentucky and Tennessee thousands of years later? No one can say for sure. It may be that generation after generation of descendants of those first Asian hunters who crossed the land bridge pushed farther south until ultimately their descendants— the Paleo-Indians—arrived in this region. After all, Paleo-Indian culture is similar to Upper Paleolithic cultures found across Asia (39). Theoretically it is possible, then, that the first humans in the Big South Fork country descended from Asian Ice Age hunters. Indeed, in our recent history, later migrants from Europe to eastern North America densely populated this continent all the way to California in a mere five hundred years.

The Paleo-Indians, the first humans in the Big South Fork country, existed in a time remote from our own, stretching back into murky prehistory. They left a paucity of clues about their existence on this continent, probably because of their constant mobility and small numbers in this area. Archaeologists, who know the Paleo-Indians by their large, two-surfaced, lance-shaped spearpoints (Hudson 1976, 39; Des Jean and Benthall 1994, 95–98), give these spearpoints such names as Clovis, Cumberland, Beaver Lake, and Quad (Hudson 1976, 42; Des Jean and Benthall 1994, 96). Some of these spearpoints have been found in the Big South Fork area, indicating that the Paleo people passed through, if only in small numbers, hunting and gathering the food resources of the area.

These mysterious Paleo-Indians were not the only early human inhabitants. Archaeologists tell us that later cultural traditions were represented here, meaning that the human inhabitants of later, but still ancient, cultural periods adapted to newer Stone Age technologies, much as we modern folk have progressed from Morse Code to the Internet. These later people fashioned different spearpoints, some smaller and differing in style from those of the Paleo-Indians (Hudson 1976, 44–45; Lewis and Kneberg 1958, 21; Des Jean and Benthall 1994, 98–107). Based upon such differences, these later people are classified as belonging to *Archaic* culture (much as we modern Americans differ culturally from, say, George Washington's eighteenth-century countrymen). Archaic culture is ancient, too, starting as far back as ten thousand years ago (Hudson 1976, 44; Lewis and Kneberg 1958, 21; Des Jean and Benthall 1994, 103).

The Archaic Indians were hunters and gatherers who seasonally used the thousands of rockshelters in the Big South Fork area
as temporary abodes. We know this because they left behind
spearpoints, bones, and charcoal from their ancient fireplaces.
Whereas there is a general paucity of Paleo-Indian stone material
in the BSFNRRA, Archaic Period cultures are well represented
there (Des Jean and Benthall 1994, 98; Des Jean 1998, personal
communication).

Following the Archaic tradition, technical and agricultural ad-
vances produced a later cultural category called the *Woodland* period. Woodland people made and used pottery or ceramics extensively, they adopted the use of the bow and arrow, and they started
burying their dead (Lewis and Kneberg 1958:32). In the Big South
Fork area, when Woodland burials were made, these generally occurred in rockshelters (Des Jean 1998, personal communication). It
is believed that agriculture became important in the lifestyle of the
Woodland people (Hudson 1976, 59). They gathered and stored
edible plants to supplement their diet of wild meat. Again, their time
here is evident in the remains they left behind.

After the Woodland period came a period archaeologists call
the *Mississippian*. The Mississippian cultural tradition is not well
represented in Big South Fork country. By the time of this tradition, some two thousand years ago, native people had moved to
the lower river valleys and were intensively engaged in agriculture.
Consequently, hunting forays into the mountains became less
necessary and less frequent.

Later, historic tribes that we call the Shawnee and the Cherokee moved in and out of Big South Fork country. They are the
aboriginal people whom the first Euro-Americans, such as Kaspar
Mansker and his party of longhunters, encountered about 1769
(Perry 1983, 65–68; Manning 1994, 77). The longhunters (so
called because of the extensive time periods required for their
hunts) made tentative forays into this country looking for animals.
In those days, a white man could make a small fortune back in
the Virginia and Carolina settlements from a year's hunt for furs
and hides (Perry 1983, 67). These longhunters returned to their
settlements with stories of the western lands across the mountains,
and their tales eventually inspired many a restless soul to seek a
fortune beyond the Cumberland Gap (Perry 1983, 69). Thus a new
people arrived, drawn by the natural resources of the area just as
the Native Americans before them had been.

The earliest extractive industry in the area was niter mining,
according to National Park Service archaeologist Tom Des Jean.
Niter mining, or mining of saltpeter, provided an ingredient used

in making gunpowder. Niter mining occurred in at least a dozen sites in the Big South Fork area from the late eighteenth century up to the Civil War (Des Jean 1998, personal communication). Oil and natural gas exploitation has also occurred in the area.

The natural resources of the area, however, were to prove its worst enemies. Mixed with the shales and sandstones of the Pennsylvanian Period rock is bituminous coal, the rock that burns. In the Carboniferous Period three hundred million years ago, nature had converted swamps, bogs, and wetlands into a resource that the energy-hungry world of the nineteenth and twentieth centuries could use.

The area also had great stands of old-growth forest. In the last years of the 1890s, a Michigan timber merchant sent his agent down to buy up land in the South Fork country. A sixty-year boom commenced. In time, Justus Stearns and his agents started a timber and railroad operation—ultimately called the Stearns Coal and Lumber Company—in Scott, Pickett, and Fentress counties in Tennessee, and in what later would become McCreary County, Kentucky (Perry 1983, 203–17). They soon found out that, in addition to wood, the area possessed a form of black gold—not oil, but coal. Coal was needed to fuel the steam locomotives bringing out the timber, and coal itself could be sold. Coal became king, and the Stearns coal towns pushed farther out into the wilderness of Big South Fork country.

Blue Heron Mine Tipple. Photograph by Arthur McDade.

Supply and market forces changed, as they do with all natural resources. By the last third of this century, the coal mining and timber harvesting slowly came to a halt. When the Stearns Company left the area in the 1970s, much of the land was spoiled and denuded. Abandoned coal camps, logging roads, and railroad tracks were left behind as reminders of the boom and bust.

Local people carried on with their lives as best they could after the coal years ended. Some found work elsewhere; some continued to farm, fish, hunt, and use the area. When the timber and mining operations stopped, the forest got a chance to grow back, and the river got a respite from siltation and acid runoff. A new breed of resource user started to visit the area: backpackers, canoeists, kayakers, and horseback riders. The word went out that the Big South Fork area was a remote wild region, just what many urban dwellers were looking for in the early 1970s. By 1974, enough people were interested in preserving the area that Congress made it a National River and Recreation Area, administered by the National Park Service (NPS). This new federal land greatly augmented several extant public preserves: the Daniel Boone National Forest (DBNF), just over the state line in Kentucky; Pickett State Park; and Scott and Pickett state forests in Tennessee.

After the federal government acquired the wild resources of the area, visitors started to come—approximately 900,000 annually in recent years. The U.S. Army Corps of Engineers, who initially wanted a dam on the river, laid out a system of buildings, roads, and trails throughout the 125,000 authorized acres of the new preserve. The corps worked in conjunction with the NPS, which ultimately took over management. The NPS opened two visitor centers in the BSFNRRA—one at Bandy Creek, 12 miles west of Oneida, Tennessee, off Highway 297; and one just over the Tennessee-Kentucky state border, on Kentucky Highway 92 near Stearns, Kentucky. An interpretive center, providing information on the cultural history of the area, exists at Blue Heron Mine, on the Kentucky side of the border. Visitors also can get information on the area from the visitor center at Pickett State Park on Tennessee Highway 154 northeast of Jamestown, Tennessee; and from the Stearns District Ranger Office in DBNF on U.S. Highway 27, 4 miles north of Whitley City, Kentucky.

Today, the BSFNRRA encompasses 125,000 federally authorized acres along the Big South Fork of the Cumberland River. Combined with more than 100,000 acres of the Stearns and Somerset districts of the DBNF, Pickett State Park and Forest, and Scott State Forest, a zone of over 225,000 acres now is protected and invites visitors to experience its cultural and natural wonders.

Part 2
The
Landforms

THE SETTING

The landforms of the Big South Fork region lie relatively close to each other on the Northern Cumberland Plateau. This is not surprising, since the geology is generally consistent within the region. However, human beings have distributed these features within a two-state, four-agency universe. The states of Tennessee and Kentucky lay claim to them geographically, while four separate government land management agencies are charged with their protection and interpretation.

The federal government manages a vast tract of over two hundred thousand acres on the Northern Cumberland Plateau in the Big South Fork National River and Recreation Area and the Stearns and Somerset districts of Daniel Boone National Forest. This large joint federal enclave is the site of many of the arches and natural features described in this guidebook. Pickett Civilian Conservation Corps Memorial State Park and Forest in Pickett County, Tennessee, shares a boundary with both these federal preserves, adding eleven thousand more acres of Tennessee park and forest lands. Several significant arches and features are located within this area. As of this writing, plans are afoot to secure donations of land to enlarge Pickett Forest's acreage.

Together, these four land management agencies provide the protection and interpretation necessary for the appreciation of these natural features, and their combined land constitutes the geographical setting treated in this guidebook. The descriptions of arches and features which follow are grouped generally by the land management unit in which they stand. In a few cases, I have included some features in a different agency section because their location and access is nearer the other agency's boundary. Each section below begins with a short orientation to the conservation agency on whose public lands the geological features of the Big South Fork area are located.

ARCHES AND FEATURES OF THE BIG SOUTH FORK NATIONAL RIVER AND RECREATION AREA

The central area within the scope of this guidebook consists of 125,000 authorized acres managed by the National Park Service (NPS). The Big South Fork National River and Recreation Area (BSFNRRA) is not a national park like the nearby Great Smoky Mountains. Intensively exploited for timber and minerals throughout the first two-thirds of the twentieth century, the area is not a pristine wilderness of old-growth forest. In fact, precious few old-growth patches remain, in inaccessible canyons.

The forest today is regaining its natural appearance, with a hearty second-growth mixed deciduous and coniferous composition. You'll find healthy oaks and white and Virginia pines on the plateau, and a dense collection of mesophytic forest hardwoods on the canyon slopes. Here you'll see poplar, beech, maple, ash, buckeye, and broad-leaf and umbrella magnolias spreading their ample elephant-ear leaves. In the cool drainages descending from the plateau occur the hemlock trees, whose wonderful shade can provide ten degrees or more of temperature relief on hot summer days. Luxuriously girdling the hemlocks along the sloping watercourses are mountain laurel and rhododendron thickets. These blanket the hillsides. Interestingly, when I came to live in the Big South Fork area, I had to learn new names for these species. In the Big South Fork, locals call mountain laurel "ivy," and rhododendron "laurel." Descending to the zone of river and side streams, you'll encounter river beech, sweet gum, and sycamore trees. With plentiful rain and south-facing slopes, the forest is faring well.

The Big South Fork of the Cumberland River is the reference point for the BSFNRRA. Looking at the park map, one sees that the BSFNRRA has attempted to encompass the major drainages of the river system within its boundaries. Unfortunately it has not quite picked up all of them. Most of the park is located in Scott and Fentress counties of Tennessee. Some eighty thousand acres of the park lie in Tennessee, with the remaining acreage located in south-eastern Kentucky.

The park grew out of federal government efforts to build a dam for a recreational reservoir in the 1930s. The Corps of Engineers drew up plans for such a dam, projected to coordinate with others in East Tennessee and Kentucky. As noted earlier, Congress delayed approving funds for this dam. By the early 1970s, the Stearns Coal and Lumber Company and other natural-resource extractors with vast acreage in the region became willing to sell off their marginal lands. Tennessee and Kentucky congressmen led a movement to create a national park in the area. Upon further study, a different designation, "national river and recreation area," was identified as more appropriate for the area (Baker and Netherton 1993, 23–25).

Historically, the title "national park" has been reserved for areas of supreme natural significance, where important biological and botanical processes are essentially intact or can flourish readily. The Big South Fork area has been intensively exploited; the disruptive effects of human intervention are still clearly evident. Additionally, national park designation would have made it necessary to prohibit many of the uses traditionally made of the area, such as hunting, trapping, and extensive horseback riding. Thus the government elected to make this a "national recreation area" and tossed in the additional sobriquet "national river," due to the significance of the major free-flowing stream that drains the study area. This management category allowed more flexibility for managing historical uses and impacts on the land, such as hunting, trapping, fishing, horseback riding, and off-road vehicle use—all activities very popular in nearby human communities. In 1974, Congress authorized the study area's inclusion in the NPS system.

The NPS and the Corps of Engineers—two very different federal agencies—jointly began planning for the development and use of this new NPS unit. The corps used its engineering expertise in planning and building the infrastructure of the area (roads, trails, campgrounds, buildings), while the NPS set about arranging to manage land and hire personnel. With the arrival of staff, the NPS developed its interpretation of area resources and started monitoring and inventorying the biological and botanical features. The NPS also began law enforcement and maintenance activities to protect and maintain the cultural and natural resources now under its authority. This close working relationship between the Corps of Engineers and the NPS lasted until 1991, when the corps finished its construction work and handed full management of the area over to the NPS. Interestingly, the very first national park, Yellowstone, also was managed and developed by the U.S. Army and its engineering arm, from 1886 until 1916. The NPS was not created until 1916.

Today, the BSFNRRA contains two visitor centers, two modern developed campgrounds with electrical hookups, two developed horse camps, a host of roads, numerous hiking and multi-use trails, interpretive centers, and scenic overlooks. In addition to all this, Bandy Creek has a public swimming pool and horse stable. Outfitters run whitewater and flatwater excursions on the seventy-plus miles of the river system. Just outside the south boundary of the park, the historic town of Rugby, Tennessee (a failed English expatriate colony of the 1880s), is an additional attraction for those interested in history and historic architecture. A scenic railroad makes spring, summer, and fall excursions from Stearns, Kentucky (just over the Tennessee state line), down to the Blue Heron Mining Community in the park—a real treat for railroad and history buffs.

The BSFNRRA lays claim to the largest pairing of natural arches in the southeastern part of the United States and quite possibly in the entire American East. South and North Arch of Twin Arches comprise a duo of natural arches which rank with others anywhere. To view them requires a hike of only 0.8 mile (one way) from a trailhead. Several other impressive arches and features are conveniently accessible to park visitors. Split Bow Arch, Wagon Arch, Needle Arch, and Devil's Jump Overlook all require only short hikes. The park also has two fine examples of chimney rocks right off Station Camp Road; these can be seen by driving up to them.

The park area is used by almost a million visitors annually, and expectations are that use will grow in the near future. The NPS is providing needed protection and management for this area and encouraging natural processes to become dominant once again. BSFNRRA is an area of truly national significance.

Needle Arch and Slave Falls

Maps: USGS Quad Barthell, SW; KY/TN. See map 1 in this guidebook.
Hiking Distance: 1.6 miles, one way.
Directions: From the Bandy Creek Visitor Center, drive 1.5 miles to Tennessee Highway 297 via the paved Bandy Creek Road. Turn right and go west 10.5 miles to the junction with Tennessee Highway 154 at Sharp Place. Turn right (north) and travel 1.9 miles. Look for Divide Road on the right. There is also a sign here for

Needle Arch. Photograph by David Morris. Used by permission.

the Charit Creek "Hostel" or Lodge, and for the Twin Arches. Turn right onto the gravel Divide Road. Proceed past the Middle Creek Trailhead and continue for another 0.2 mile to Fork Ridge Road on the right. Turn right here and go 1.1 miles, past the Middle Creek Equestrian Trailhead, to the Sawmill Trailhead on the left. There is ample parking here.

From the Sawmill Trailhead, follow the trail behind the bulletin board. This trail immediately turns left and parallels Fork Ridge Road for a short distance before reaching the Slave Falls Loop Trail. At this junction, turn right and proceed along this latter trail. At just under a mile, you will see the Slave Falls Loop Trail bear to the right. Go straight ahead on the Slave Falls/Charit Creek Trail toward Slave Falls.

At 1.0 mile, you'll come to a trail sign indicating Slave Falls off to the left 0.2 mile. While you're in the area, be sure to take this short spur trail to this impressive 60-foot waterfall. It is worth seeing, although there will be several steep stone steps to negotiate. At the falls, you'll find a National Park Service wayside exhibit on waterfalls. After seeing the falls, retrace your steps back 0.2 mile to the main trail.

Continue on the main trail (this is the Slave Falls/Charit Creek

Slave Falls. Photograph by David Morris. Used by permission.

Trail) for an additional 0.2 mile east. The trail passes right by the Needle Arch. After seeing this delicate arch, you can return to your vehicle by merely retracing your steps past Slave Falls to return to the Sawmill Trailhead.

Description: This relatively short trail to Needle Arch is one of the nicest short day hikes in the BSFNRRA. There is much to see and do in this western "Middle Creek" section of the park. In addition to the enjoyment of seeing Needle Arch, the hiker can enjoy an easy-to-moderate loop trail which provides access to Slave Falls (a beautiful 60-foot waterfall that is well worth the short 0.2-mile detour). This trail also connects you with the Slave Falls/Charit Creek Trail, which can take you to Charit Creek Lodge, if you're looking for a longer hike or an overnight backpack. For information on backcountry trail connectors, consult the "Trails Illustrated" topographical map or one of the hiking trail guides listed in the "Selected References" section of this guidebook.

The trail from the Sawmill Trailhead to Slave Falls and Needle Arch passes through a peaceful mixed deciduous and hemlock forest and crosses a tributary of Mill Creek. Mill is one of the three creeks which make up the Middle Creek drainage, the other two being Andy Creek and Middle Creek itself. This trail brings you to one of the finest waterfalls and one of the most impressive arches in the recreation area.

At Needle Arch, you'll find a National Park Service wayside exhibit explaining how arches form (there is another wayside exhibit about natural arches at Twin Arches). Needle Arch is a graceful arch thirteen feet high and thirty-five feet wide. It is an example of a sandstone finger ridge that resulted where widening of a joint and the collapse of a rock shelter separated the arch span from the ridge. Water ran down and through the widened joint, further eroding the softer rock beneath the resistant deck of the arch, undercutting the soft sandstone, and ultimately leaving a more resistant strata of sandstone to form an arch lintel.

Needle Arch is a great place to stop awhile and maybe enjoy a small picnic or at least a daypack sandwich. There is an open area around the wayside exhibit that is perfect for this. This is a graceful arch to be savored and admired.

For your own safety and for the preservation of the arch, please do not climb up on this arch (or any of the other arches). The arch is worth saving for future visitors.

To return to the Sawmill Trailhead, retrace your steps and go back the way you came past Slave Falls to the Sawmill Trailhead.

When you get back to your vehicle, you have the option of visiting Dead Deer Arch and Twin Arches via Divide Road. To reach these arches, turn right on Divide Road and refer to the following arch descriptions for directions to these landform features.

Dead Deer Arch

Maps: USGS Quad Sharp Place, TN/KY. See map 1 in this guidebook.

Hiking Distance: 0.1 mile, one way.

Caution: *This arch is located near the edge of a cliff. Exercise extreme caution when looking for this arch and do not approach the edge of any vertical bluff. Observe this arch from below the bluff edge. Follow the directions to this arch carefully. Visiting this arch will require off-trail hiking several hundred yards down (and back up) a small gully, so it is recommended for those who are in good physical shape. This arch should be visited only in the winter months when poisonous snakes and stinging insects are not present, since it is located a short distance off-trail.*

Directions: From the Bandy Creek Visitor Center, drive 1.5 miles to Tennessee Highway 297 via the paved Bandy Creek Road. Turn right and go west 10.5 miles to the junction with Tennessee Highway 154 at Sharp Place. Turn right here. Proceed 1.9 miles to the

Dead Deer Arch.
Photograph by
David Morris. Used
by permission.

junction with Divide Road on the right (there is a sign here for Twin Arches and Charit Creek Lodge). Proceed on this gravel road past the Middle Creek Trailhead and on to the intersection with Fork Ridge Road on the right. From this intersection with Fork Ridge Road, continue on Divide Road for an additional 0.8 mile. Be sure to gauge the 0.8-mile distance from the junction with Fork Ridge Road accurately, or you may not find this arch. At precisely 0.8 mile, pull completely off the road and park (you will have to be creative about finding a parking space, but don't block the road). The top of Dead Deer Arch is 45 feet southwest from the left edge of Divide Road (to the left of where you parked).

There is no trail to this arch. Nor can you see the arch from the road. Walk to the southwest at a 45-degree angle from your vehicle into the woods. Be cautious and on the lookout for a crack two feet wide at the edge of the bluff. If you see this space, bear farther to the southwest (your left) to locate a spot where the vertical bluff ends and a moderate hill descends into the valley below. Carefully descend this hill with a large patch of rhododendron on your right. Bear to your right (north) for 40 yards around this rhododendron. You will go down a small gully and ascend its north side. Look to your right toward the bluffline. You should see a rockshelter whose entrance is shrouded in rhododendron. Proceed up the slope to the rockshelter and carefully walk to the bluff wall. Look up to the right to see the arch lintel formed by the two-foot crack.

Description: This arch is located right on the border of the BSFNRRA and Pickett State Forest. Since it is on the road leading to Twin Arches and is so close to a gravel road maintained by the National Park Service, I have included it in the section on the BSFNRRA.

Even though this arch is not located on a trail, it is only 45 feet from the western edge of Divide Road (which you have to drive to get to Twin Arches anyway). It is such an interesting feature that it warrants inclusion in this guidebook. Since there is no trail to this arch feature, I highly recommend visiting it only in winter (in spring, summer and fall, you may be annoyed—or harmed— by snakes, ticks, and vegetation).

Even though this arch is so close to a park road, it can be hard to find. It is probably the most challenging of all the landforms in this guide. If you were driving on Divide Road and didn't know about it, you wouldn't suspect that only a few feet from the side of the road, this geological feature exists. You have to view it from below the bluffline in order to appreciate it.

Pickett State Park Ranger David Delk and Bob Wheeley, a local river guide and explorer, tell the following story to account for this arch's name. Some hunters once were on Divide Road when they smelled something rotten. Inspecting the area to locate the source of the smell, they discovered that a deer had fallen through the crack in the bluff. Its carcass could be seen on the floor of the rockshelter beneath the crack.

This arch is a great example of widening of a joint. You can see the delicate space separating the main cliffline from this arch span. This arch appears to have been formed recently; the lines of the rocks in the arch and at the top of the crack have sharp edges and have not been rounded off by long-term erosion. The space between the main bluff and the arch lintel is small, too—another clue that the separation of this span from the mother bluff was rather recent, at least in geological terms. The rock breakdown at the bottom of the arch also suggests a recent origin.

This arch is difficult to measure, since it is hard to decide where to stand on the breakdown beneath the lintel. It is estimated to be eighteen feet high and forty feet wide.

Dead Deer Arch is located within a few miles of Twin Arches and Needle Arch and is not very far from Natural Bridge in Pickett State Park. It is a little more difficult to get to without a trail, but it is well worth the extra effort.

Be careful as you retrace your steps out of the rockshelter and up the gully back to Divide Road.

From Divide Road, you can continue north to the turnoff to Twin Arches, just a few miles distant, and visit those amazing landforms. Refer to the following section for directions.

Twin Arches

Maps: USGS Quad Barthell SW, KY/TN. See map 1 in this guidebook.

Hiking Distance: 0.8 mile, one way.

Directions: From the Bandy Creek Visitor Center, drive 1.5 miles to Tennessee Highway 297 via the paved Bandy Creek Road. Turn right on 297 and proceed west for 10.5 miles to the junction with Tennessee Highway 154 at Sharp Place. Turn right and go north on Highway 154 for 1.9 miles to Divide Road on the right, which is marked with a reflective street sign. At this junction, there are also signs for the Charit Creek Lodge and for Twin Arches. From

South Arch, Twin Arches. Photograph by David Morris. Used by permission.

here it is 4 miles on a gravel road to the turnoff to Twin Arches Trail. The road is hard-packed gravel, but it can have potholes. Turn onto Divide Road and proceed past the Middle Creek Trailhead. Continue straight. You'll reach a junction with Fork Ridge Road on the right. At this junction, there is a sign pointing straight ahead for Twin Arches. Continue straight on Divide Road.

While you're passing this way, you may want to make a side excursion to Dead Deer Arch, which will be coming up on your left in 0.8 mile from the junction with Fork Ridge Road. Read the arch description (above) for Dead Deer Arch before attempting to find this arch, however, and note that there is no trail to it. It is recommended for winter, when no snakes will be present. At the junction with Fork Ridge Road, you can also turn right to visit Needle Arch (see description of this arch in this guidebook).

To get to Twin Arches Road, however, proceed straight ahead on Divide Road past the junction with Fork Ridge Road. Continuing on Divide Road, in approximately 2.7 miles you will see a sign for the Twin Arches Road. Turn right here and follow this road 2.1 miles to the trailhead. From there it is a hike of only 0.8 mile down to Twin Arches. The trail can be strenuous, depending on the shape you're in, with some stairs and climbing both going in and coming back. You'll drop approximately 300 feet in elevation down to the arches, with a corresponding rise on the way out.

Description: The most impressive natural arches in the Big South Fork area—and arguably in the eastern United States—are the Twin Arches. These large natural arches sometimes are referred to locally as "Double Arches" or "Tandem Arches." Corgan and Parks, in *The Natural Bridges of Tennessee,* also call them "Double Arches." The official name is Twin Arches.

"In most dimensions South Arch is the larger of the two. Each arch is a major topographic feature," say Corgan and Parks. The National Park Service has prepared an interpretive site bulletin on Twin Arches which states that South Arch has a deck "103 feet high with a clearance of about 70 feet. North Arch, in contrast, has a height of about 62 feet with a 51-foot clearance." These are the dimensions given by Corgan and Parks. The authors of *Hiking the Big South Fork* (1999) give the following dimensions for Twin Arches: "The larger South Arch has a clearance of 70 feet and a span of over 135 feet. The North Arch has a 51-foot clearance and a 93-foot span" (79–81).

The two arches are part of the same finger ridge, which defines two separate drainages. Headward erosion on both sides of the ridge over eons of time has carved out the less resistant sandstone beneath the lintels of the arches, producing a nearly perfect arch shape in each (Corgan and Parks 1979, 75). These two related arches are the largest in Tennessee and are taller than Natural Arch in Kentucky (described elsewhere in this guidebook). Even though a definitive survey of all states is unavailable, it is generally believed that only the Natural Bridge in Virginia is taller (that bridge has a taller clearance but a smaller span than South Arch). These twin arches clearly are the Big South Fork region's premier geological features. They are things of beauty which should not be missed. If you have time to visit only one arch area, make it the Twin Arches.

Also of interest at Twin Arches is the fascinating evidence of an ancestral third arch, now eroded away (Manning 1994, 47). Geologists believe that, at one time, there was another arch south of South Arch. This is suggested by a space at the southern end of the ridgeline which contains North and South Arch; a breakdown pile indicates the possible collapse of an ancestral arch. It is tantalizing to think that, at one time, three major arches may have occupied the same ridge.

As if Twin Arches were not sufficiently intriguing alone, two tunnels traverse the bases of the arches (Corgan and Parks 1979, 75). Beneath South Arch lies what is called West Tunnel. It is a tight, 88-foot passageway through the base of South Arch. After maneuvering through it, you can turn left and return on the east side to South Arch. There is also a small breezeway, flatteringly called East Tunnel, right below the wooden staircase between the two arches. This is a very small crawlway but nevertheless an interesting feature in the area.

Perhaps no other arch area offers so much access to other backcountry attractions as Twin Arches. There are several wonderful trails for day trips or overnight backpacking. For an excellent day hike, if you are in good shape, consider taking the entire Twin Arches/Charit Creek Loop Trail, a moderate to strenuous 5.5-mile hike with some uphill climbing. The Twin Arches/Charit Creek Loop takes the hiker past rock alcoves used by ancient Indian hunters (one of these alcoves has an interesting chimney hole). The trail passes seasonal waterfalls, an abandoned historic farmstead known as "Jake's Place," and Charit Creek Lodge, a quaint, rustic backcountry lodge nestled in the beautiful valleys of Charit and Station Camp creeks. Overnight accommodations and meals can be arranged through the lodge by telephoning (423) 429-5704. Reservations are required.

Jake's Place, the deserted and forlorn homestead of Jacob

Blevins, Jr., and his wife Viannah, is 1.3 miles from Charit Creek Lodge and is on the Twin Arches/Charit Creek Loop. Only a pile of rocks from a chimney and a clearing now remain at the site, which dates from the 1880s. Part of the west bunkhouse cabin at Charit Creek Lodge was built of logs from Jake's Place.

Charit Creek Lodge has served as a hunting lodge (operated by Joe Simpson as the Parch Corn Creek Hunting Camp), a youth hostel, and now a rustic backcountry lodge (Manning 1994, 78–83).

The Twin Arches/Charit Creek Loop can be started at the North Arch, or at the Charit Creek Lodge 1.1 miles to the south from Twin Arches. You also can reach Charit Creek Lodge from the Fork Ridge Road off Divide Road in the west-central part of the park. It is only 0.8 mile from the Charit Creek Trailhead to the lodge. For a longer hike to Charit Creek Lodge, take the Slave Falls Loop Trail (this trail starts at Sawmill Trailhead on Fork Ridge Road) and connect with the Slave Falls–Charit Creek Trail. For hiking options in the area and throughout the park, consult the "Trails Illustrated" topo map or one of the published trail guides listed in the "Selected References" section of this guidebook.

In all of the Big South Fork country, the area in and around Charit Creek and Twin Arches is a popular favorite. The Twin Arches, the geological rockhouses with their history of human occupation in ancient times, and the cultural history of the early pioneers make this area unsurpassed for beauty and history. If you have to pick only one area to visit in the Big South Fork backcountry, make it the Twin Arches/Charit Creek region.

Chimney Rocks (Station Camp Road)

Maps: USGS Quad Oneida North and Barthell SW, TN/KY. See map 2 in this guidebook.
Hiking Distance: 50 feet, one way.
Directions: From the Bandy Creek Visitor Center, drive 1.5 miles to Tennessee Highway 297 via the paved Bandy Creek Road. Turn left and go east 8.9 miles to the stop sign at the junction of Highway 297 and Station Camp Road. In the process of driving to this location, you'll drop down into the canyon of the Big South Fork of the Cumberland River, cross the river at Leatherwood Ford, and continue on up out of the gorge until you come to a stop sign at the Terry and Terry grocery store at the junction of Highway 297 and Station Camp Road.

Directly ahead, you'll see a sign pointing left to the Station Camp Horse Camp. Turn left. Proceed 4 miles, at which point

*Chimney Rock,
Station Camp.
Photograph by
Arthur McDade.*

you'll cross the boundary into the BSFNRRA again. The pavement ends here, and the road becomes a hard gravel composition. In another 0.4 mile, you'll come to a sign pointing right to the horse camp and left to the "River Access." Go left toward the river. Continue on the gravel road as it starts to descend for 2.5 miles. There you'll see a large pullout on your right, along with a sign saying "Chimney Rocks." Park here. The two chimney rocks can be seen directly across the road on the side of the hill.

Description: These two natural chimney rocks are geological features unique in the Big South Fork country. They stand out as gnarled natural sentinels on the old road to Station Camp. This area is of historical importance as well. In the latter part of the eighteenth century, "longhunters" reportedly used the area as a camp or "station" during their hunting forays into the Big South Fork region. There is also some speculation that militia, or "home guards," used the area as a camp in the Civil War era. Just down the road from the rock sentinels is Station Camp Ford, a place where the Big South Fork of the Cumberland River can be forded in low-water periods.

People have camped and forded the river on hunting and horseback trips into the area for hundreds of years. One can only imagine what these early white settlers, and the much earlier Native American passersby, thought of these strange rock formations.

A community called Station Camp formerly existed near these rock formations. These rock features were called "salt and pepper shakers" by some people, due to their shape and close proximity to each other, like shakers on a tabletop. Conley Blevins, retired schoolteacher and former NPS employee, provided me with a copy of the *Knoxville Journal* for June 5, 1949, in which a photo of one of these chimney rocks appeared in a feature article entitled "The Country Beyond." The subtitle describes the area: "Roadless, Bridgeless, and Storeless, Station Camp Has Real Mountain People." According to the photo's caption, the rocks were called "Satan's Chimney" by the local inhabitants. The newspaper account describes one of the chimney rocks as follows: "When the wind whistles through the caves at its base on dark nights, folks who have heard it will tell you it sounds like the devil is stoking his furnace."

From the Chimney Rocks parking area, you can get a nice view of the two chimneys only forty to fifty feet up the hillside on the south side of the road. There are unofficial trails, not maintained, that lead up to the chimneys, although I do not recommend using them, due to safety and resource preservation concerns. You can view these chimney rocks quite nicely from the parking lot below. The west chimney is the larger of the two, being fifteen feet high, while the east rock is eight and a half feet high. The chimneys have irregular columns with pockets of differential erosion exposed on them. Each is topped with a resistant sandstone cap. This capstone of resistant sandstone has iron mixed into it, and this fortified it against the erosion that wore away the neighboring sedimentary rock. These chimneys are the remains of sandstone strata that have eroded away around them, leaving only these resistant columns as reminders of ancient sedimentary rocks in the vicinity.

These chimney rocks are convenient roadside landforms. They are really neat natural features, looking like something you'd more likely see in Arches or Zion national parks in Utah than in the eastern plateau country. They are well worth the effort required to see them. You can turn around at the Chimney Rocks parking area and reverse your route back to Tennessee Highway 297, or you can continue another one mile down to the Big South Fork of the Cumberland River at Station Camp Creek. This is a dead-end road, but you can turn around at the parking lot at the end of the road and come back to Highway 297.

Split Bow Arch

Maps: USGS Quad Barthell, KY. See map 3 in this guidebook.
Hiking Distance: 0.7 mile loop trail.
Directions: From the NPS Visitor Center on Kentucky Highway 92 at Stearns, Kentucky, follow the directional signs for Bear Creek and Blue Heron (this route will take you on Kentucky routes 92, 1651, and 742). After 5.5 miles, you will come to an NPS directional sign on the left for the Bear Creek Scenic Area at the junction of Kentucky Highway 742 and Ross Road (Kentucky Highway 1470). Turn left here and go 3.1 miles to the southwest. The road is asphalt but turns into gravel toward the park boundary. Continue until you approach a sign for the Bear Creek Horse Camp. Turn left here; do not go right toward the horse camp. In another 0.2 mile, you'll come to the Split Bow Arch Overlook on your right.

You can park here and take a look at the arch below. To reach the trail to the arch, however, drive on another 0.2 mile straight ahead to the Bear Creek Overlook parking area. The trailhead for the short 0.7-mile Split Bow Arch Loop Trail is here. This is a moderate trail on a gentle grade down to the arch. The NPS has

Split Bow Arch.
Photograph by
Arthur McDade.

constructed wooden stairs through the arch. Follow the trail
through the arch, and it will loop back to the parking lot for the
Bear Creek Overlook.

Description: Split Bow Arch, a large arch, is unusual because it is
the result of a combination of forces. It is an active arch, too, with
seasonal water flowing through its span. Widening of a joint played
a large part in its formation. It is possible that Split Bow Arch at one
time was a rockshelter. In the distant past, a crack developed in the
sandstone at the rear of the alcove. Surface water flowing toward
the bluffline was intercepted by this crack, even as it is today; water
still seeps behind and through this arch. Water flowed down into the
crack and widened it until a large gap developed, creating a ridge
disconnected from the main bluffline. Runoff drained into the space
and undercut the less resistant sandstone below the separated ridge,
possibly weakening the rear of the rockshelter and causing a collapse.
You can see the breakdown pile beneath the arch today, suggesting
that an impressive geological event occurred. Over thousands of
years, water erosion continued to fall off the main bluffline, down
into the crack now expanded by the collapse, and through the
separated ridge, producing this fine arch.

As you approach the arch, the trail takes you through a narrow
defile, the legacy of the widened joint. This defile provides a good
study area for observing the separation of the arch ridge from the
main bluff on the right. Split Bow Arch is 33 feet, 6 inches high
from the center of the rock jumble beneath it and 51 feet wide at
its base (Daniel Boone National Forest measurements).

You can retrace your steps to return to your vehicle or continue
hiking on the Split Bow Arch Loop Trail, which will return you
to the Bear Creek Overlook parking lot for a total loop of only
0.7 mile.

While in the area, be sure to visit the Bear Creek Overlook for
what is arguably the best view of the river and its canyon in the
Big South Fork area. It is only 0.3 mile west from the Bear Creek
Overlook parking lot. To get to the overlook from the parking lot,
follow the sign which points you across a field on an old roadway
until you arrive at the treeline to the west. Continue on this trail
into the woods for 200 yards to a wooden platform, which
contains an interpretive wayside exhibit dealing with the Big South
Fork of the Cumberland River.

From this overlook, one can get a bird's-eye view of the great
erosion work that the Big South Fork of the Cumberland River
has performed in carving out the river gorge 400 feet below. To
your left from this platform is the drainage of Bear Creek, which

used to be an access point for a gauging station on the river. From this perch on a bend in the river, one can look far upstream into the mists of this ancient river and follow its progress downstream until it is lost in the meanders of the river canyon. Across the river, an endless forest with no sign of man's presence extends to the western horizon. This viewpoint is an exceptional sunset vista, but it is appealing at any time of day.

While in the area, you can return to Kentucky Highway 742 (also known as Mine 18 Road) and turn left to reach both New and Wagon arches, and Cracks-in-the-Rock. See the following sections of this guidebook for directions to these nearby features.

New Arch

Maps: USGS Quad Barthell, KY. See map 3 in this guidebook.
Hiking Distance: 150 feet, one way.
Directions: From the NPS Visitor Center at Stearns, Kentucky, go west 1 mile on Kentucky Highway 92. Here you'll see a sign directing you to bear left on Kentucky Highway 1651 toward Bear Creek and Blue Heron. Go 1 mile on Highway 1651 to the junction with Kentucky Highway 742. Turn right here and proceed 3.5 miles to the sign for the Bear Creek Scenic Area. Go past this sign and continue straight on Kentucky Highway 742 past this junction for another 1.4 miles. Look for a cemetery on your right with headstones for Stephens, Foster, and Stevens.

From this cemetery, it is only a short distance to New Arch. Proceed straight ahead past two roads on your right. In another 0.1 mile, look for a pullout on the left with a gated entrance. Pull in here and park. New Arch is 150 feet west on the other side of the road cut. Be careful of traffic on the road.

Description: New Arch is a classic example of a developing arch. It is a textbook specimen easily accessible on the side of the road. When the Mine 18 Road (Kentucky Highway 742) was constructed, the bulldozer exposed this example of a developing arch. In addition to this arch, just down the road 0.5 mile is Wagon Arch.

At New Arch, you can clearly see the arch lintel composed of harder rock, with softer rock and siltstone material still intact beneath it. The processes of erosion have been speeded up by the exposure of this arch during road construction, and they are hard at work on this exposed feature right now. Ultimately, the softer material will erode out, leaving a small lintel beside the road.

This "new" arch has an additional attraction: a smaller arch is developing on the left base of the arch, measuring approximately three feet wide and two feet high. Thus this is a double feature.

New Arch. Photograph by Arthur McDade.

As mentioned in the introduction, road cuts provide geologists with portals into the earth's strata. Even though this arch's development process has been quickened by the bulldozer's work, this is undeniably a great example of the processes of erosion which form arches.

This developing arch is on the public right-of-way on Kentucky Highway 742 and is highly accessible. I have included it in the section on the BSFNRRA, since it is only 0.5 mile from both Wagon Arch and the park boundary. It also is on the road that leads to the Devil's Jump Overlook and Blue Heron in the BSFNRRA. Since it has no official name and is a developing natural arch, I have termed it "New" for identification purposes in this guidebook.

Wagon Arch

Maps: USGS Quad Barthell, KY. See map 3 in this guidebook.
Hiking Distance: 50 yards, one way.
Directions: From the NPS Visitor Center at Stearns, Kentucky, follow the signs toward Blue Heron (Kentucky Highway 92 to Kentucky Highway 1651, and then to Kentucky Highway 742). On the way to Wagon Arch, be sure to pull off the road and see

Wagon Arch.
Photograph by
Arthur McDade .

New Arch, which is being formed right beside the highway (see above).

When you pass the "Entering Big South Fork NRRA" sign on Kentucky Highway 742, go 0.4 mile farther. Look for Wagon Arch on the right, slightly above you on a curve in the road. Since Wagon Arch is located right off the road, please don't stop or park in the road directly in front of it; there is a pulloff area just east from the arch on the left side of the road. You will have to drive past the arch and turn around to reach the parking area off the road. Be very careful of traffic on the road when you walk over to see the arch.

Description: Wagon Arch is one of the most accessible of all the arches in the Big South Fork region, being even closer to the road than Natural Bridge in Pickett State Park. Located right on the north side of paved Kentucky Highway 742 (Mine 18 Road), it is a delicate and graceful span of rock.

This arch is actually on land in the Daniel Boone National Forest, but, from the location of the BSFNRRA entrance sign on

Kentucky Highway 742, it appears to be on National Park Service land. Actually, the arch lies 0.1 mile outside the NPS boundary. For ease of reference, however, I have included it in the BSFNRRA section since it is barely outside the official boundary of the park, and it is on the road to features in the park—the river gorge overlooks and Cracks-in-the-Rock. It also is relatively near Split Bow Arch and Bear Creek Overlook. A trip to Wagon Arch opens up opportunities for observing other natural and cultural attractions in the vicinity.

This arch's official name on the inventory of Daniel Boone National Forest arches is "Wagon Arch." It is also commonly referred to as "Wagon Wheel Arch."

Wagon Arch, by one account, got its name from the horse-drawn wagons that traveled by—and over—it in the past, prior to the construction of the new Mine 18 Road (Kentucky Highway 742). I have heard that this arch had to be supported by wooden beams during construction of Mine 18 Road into the park, for fear that the road machinery's vibrations might bring it down. Fortunately, care was taken, and this small but graceful arch survived.

Wagon Arch is 12 feet, 8 inches high and 34 feet wide at its base (these are the official measurements of the Daniel Boone National Forest and were taken from the north side of the arch, not from the Highway 742 side). You can walk down under the arch to the north side, but watch your step; there are no steps or stairs. Watch out, too, for poison ivy; it flourishes under the arch.

This arch formed through the collapse of a rockshelter which faced north, away from the road; from Highway 742, one actually looks through the rear of the ancestral rockshelter. The rock rubble beneath the arch lintel is evidence of a collapse. The arch is located on a narrow finger ridge which has been dissected by highway construction. For sheer convenience, this arch can't be beat.

While in the area, check out the views of the canyon of the Big South Fork of the Cumberland River on the River Gorge Overlooks Road, a half-mile farther west on the left off Highway 742. Devil's Jump Overlook affords a spectacular panoramic view of the geology of the Big South Fork river canyon. You look across at sheer sandstone bluffs on the opposite side of the river, with overhangs produced as huge blocks of rock fell from the bluff into the river four hundred feet below. Looking down at Devil's Jump Rapid, you can see sandstone boulders the size of houses. These have fallen down from the west bluff into the river, creating a major whitewater rapid. Devil's Jump Rapid occurs in a mild downstream section of the river, with a small drop per mile. Colluvial breakdown from the bluff walls above, however, blocks the river at this point, creating a boiling whitewater cauldron. Such erosion of major blocks continues to expand the width of the river canyon, demonstrating that the Big South Fork of the Cumberland River is still an active agent of geological change.

Several other fascinating features occur near the Devil's Jump Overlook parking area. If you take a short hike north toward Cracks-in-the-Rock, you can see a complex of fifteen dwarf column arches right along the trail. Cracks-in-the-Rock itself is an amazing natural feature in which huge sandstone blocks have shifted from the bluff wall, creating a cavelike passage (see description of Cracks-in-the-Rock elsewhere in this guidebook).

While in the area, take time to visit the historic coal-mining communities of Barthell and Blue Heron, located a couple of miles on down Highway 742 (also called Mine 18 Road and Blue Heron Road). Blue Heron is an open-air interpretive museum and is available to the public free of charge.

Blue Heron was a coal-mining town of the Stearns Coal and Lumber Company. It operated from 1938 until 1962, when it was shut down. It fell into disrepair and ultimately became a ghost town. In 1974, the area became part of the BSFNRRA, and Blue Heron was renovated to serve as an outdoor museum. Visitors can roam the town freely, visiting buildings and listening to taped reminiscences of people who actually lived and worked at Blue Heron. It is possible to walk over a coal tipple bridge a thousand feet long and enter the façade of one of the Blue Heron mines, where mannequins dressed as coal miners evoke the heyday of life in this company town. Don't miss Blue Heron.

The nearby coal town of Barthell is also well worth a visit. Barthell was the site of the first coal mine for the Stearns Coal and Lumber Company in 1902. This town ultimately had several hundred workers and residents, and it had a store, a post office, and a school. By the 1960s, Barthell was closed down. Like Blue Heron, it became a ghost town. Local developer Harold Koger and his wife Marilyn Koger are reconstructing Barthell. The town opened in summer 1998 as a stop on the scenic railway out of Stearns, Kentucky, and for overnight lodging and dining. This town is on private property and not on National Park Service or Daniel Boone National Forest land.

Cracks-in-the-Rock

Maps (including Dwarf Column Arches): USGS Quad, Barthell, KY. See map 3 in this guidebook.
Hiking Distance: 0.6 mile, one way.
Directions: From the NPS Visitor Center off Highway 92 in

Cracks-in-the-Rock. Photograph by Arthur McDade.

Stearns, Kentucky, go west on Highway 92 for 1 mile until you come to the junction with Kentucky Highway 1651. There is a brown-and-white sign here pointing left for Bear Creek and Blue Heron. Bear left here. Continue on Highway 1651 for another mile, until you see a sign pointing right at Revelo, Kentucky, for Blue Heron and Bear Creek on Kentucky Highway 742. Turn right here. Follow Highway 742 past New and Wagon arches (see descriptions of these features in this guidebook). Go past the entrance to the Blue Heron campground. A half-mile past the campground, you'll see a sign pointing left for the River Gorge Overlooks. Turn left here. Go 1.1 miles on this road to the second parking area on your left. This is the Devil's Jump Overlook parking area. Park here. The trail to Cracks-in-the-Rock starts on the right near the sign showing a red arrowhead (this is the symbol for foot trails in the BSFNRRA). The trail from the Devil's Jump parking area is a continuation of the 6.5-mile Blue Heron Loop Trail. This trail to Cracks-in-the-Rock involves seventy-three steps to descend and then ascend. It can be strenuous. But if you are healthy and in shape, the short hike to this feature is a pleasant experience.

Description: This short hike to Cracks-in-the-Rock along a segment of the Blue Heron Loop Trail is a delightful combination of interesting geological features. From the parking lot, you can make a short hike along the paved trail to the left to the Devil's Jump Overlook for an incredible view of the canyon of the Big South Fork of the Cumberland River. Or you can start out immediately on the Blue Heron Loop Trail to the right, which leads you to Cracks-in-the-Rock.

If you elect to visit the overlook first, you'll look out over one of the best views in the Big South Fork country. Here you'll see the geology of the country in action, as the Big South Fork of the Cumberland River cuts its way through the canyon. It is still working at sculpting this terrain, as is shown by the large blocks of sandstone which clog the river below, forming a major whitewater rapid called Devil's Jump. If you look at the rock wall above the rapid on the west side, you'll see overhangs where great blocks of sandstone have fallen off into the river below. Who knows when these blocks crashed off their vertical perches into the river? It is conceivable that new blocks could fall at any time, further constricting the river channel and enlarging the already large canyon here and elsewhere. During high-water periods, I have seen the great blocks of sandstone which form the Devil's Jump Rapid completely covered by floodwater, making huge boils and holes comparable to the rapids in the Colorado River in the Grand Canyon.

From the observation deck at the overlook, you can see the level profile of the Cumberland Plateau in three directions. If you could fill in the river canyon, the east side of the river where you stand would be on the same plane as the west side. The river has carved out this gorge and continues to carve it out, even as you look down upon it.

You can return to the parking lot and continue north on the Blue Heron Loop Trail where there is a sign for "Cracks-in-the-Rock." This trail starts out level, as it parallels the bluffline. It makes its way through a shaded forest, past rock bluffs on the right where rockshelters are visible. As you round a bend to the right at 0.2 mile, you can see the gorge of the Big South Fork of the Cumberland River and start to hear the roar of the Devil's Jump Rapid 400 feet below you. The trail now starts to hug the bluff, with the canyon opening up for view on your left. You'll pass directly beneath the Gorge Overlook pavilion at 0.4 mile. Walk on another 100 feet, looking for a holly tree near a sandstone rock on the right side of the trail.

Directly below this rock is a miniature alcove with "dwarf column arches" forming at the base. They are located right along the trail at waist height. You have to be on the lookout to spot them. They appear as pockets of erosion in the sandstone rock, and there are at least fifteen separate column arches of varying small sizes, ranging from a half-inch to two feet. These small arches are a microcosm of the arch world of the Big South Fork country. In just the same way larger arches are formed, they are forming as the softer sandstone around them is being eroded by seeping water percolating down from the bluff above. They look like a fairyland grotto, in which you might imagine dwarves or elves appearing. Granted, these are small rock features, but they provide a wonderful opportunity to visualize the formation of arches in general.

If you reach the signboard showing "Cracks-in-the-Rock" and "Blue Heron" at a trail junction without seeing the dwarf column arches, you have gone too far. Turn around and retrace your steps for 200 feet. The small column arches are just around the bend on the left of the trail.

After viewing the dwarf arches, continue north toward Cracks-in-the-Rock on the red arrowhead trail (Blue Heron Loop Trail) past a trail signboard at 0.5 mile. The trail makes a swing to the left and descends to a set of steep wooden stairs leading down a rock defile. There are seventy-three of these steps (including some water-bar logs which form steps at the bottom), and they can be slippery. After carefully descending the steps, you'll be on the next bench of the bluffline, and the trail will take you several hundred feet farther to a sign showing "Cracks-in-the-Rock." Go another 100 feet past the signboard, and the trail starts to enter a rock passageway with stone and wooden steps. This is Cracks-in-the-Rock.

Cracks-in-the-Rock was formed by the partial fracturing of several huge blocks of sandstone on the top bluffline. These blocks cracked, shifted, and leaned into each other, creating passageways through spaces left in the breakdown. Additional rockfall between the spaces enlarged the passageways, creating a cavelike appearance. Weathering and erosion constantly are at work on the rock bluffs, causing blocks to shift or collapse from the main bluff at times, much as the great blocks of rock in the river at Devil's Jump Rapid did. The huge blocks at Cracks-in-the-Rock had support from the bench slope beneath them, and this prevented them from separating completely from the bluff and tumbling four hundred feet down into the river canyon.

Walk carefully up the steps to the wooden platform in the passageway and see rays of light coming through the slits in the rock. Three distinct "cracks" are visible here, and they form passageways through these huge sandstone blocks. The trail passes through these blocks and descends wooden steps twenty feet to a

level "room." Walk to the end of this room and turn around to
see the great cracks and fissures between the huge blocks of
sandstone. Imagine the erosional forces working all along the
bluffline in the Big South Fork canyon system. Places like Cracks-
in-the-Rock and Maude's Crack (another passageway through
sandstone blocks, located west of the Big South Fork of the
Cumberland River in Tennessee) illustrate the great forces of
erosion and gravity at work in this sedimentary landscape. It is
indeed a dynamic geological system, one even now carving this
land into new shapes.

You can retrace your steps back up to the Devil's Jump
Overlook parking lot or continue downhill to Blue Heron Mine
(you'll need to have a vehicle shuttled there to meet you). Or you
can continue on the entire 6.5-mile Blue Heron Loop, which will
take you through the Blue Heron Mining Community, then along
the river past Devil's Jump Rapid, and ultimately back to your
vehicle at the Devil's Jump Overlook. This loop trail takes three
to five hours and can be strenuous. If you decide to take the entire
loop, follow the red arrowhead signs on the trees. In May through
October, you can get water and cold drinks from vending machines
at the snack bar at the Blue Heron Mining Community, where
there is also a pay phone.

ARCHES AND FEATURES OF PICKETT STATE PARK AND FOREST

Pickett State Park and Forest is a preserve managed jointly by two state agencies. The park is operated by the State Parks Division of the Tennessee Department of Environment and Conservation, and the forest by the Tennessee Division of Forestry.

The preserve shares the geology of the Big South Fork area, being adjacent to both the Big South Fork National River and Recreation Area and the Daniel Boone National Forest. The state park's actual title now is Pickett Civilian Conservation Corps Memorial State Park; but the old title, Pickett State Park, is commonly used.

Pickett State Park and Forest contain a surprising number of noteworthy arches and other geological features in close proximity to each other along Tennessee Highway 154. This proximity allows an energetic and physically fit visitor to visit all the key features in one trip. Moreover, the park's trail system offers varied hiking and backpacking opportunities amid a relaxed atmosphere with rustic lodging in the Tennessee hills. Some of Pickett's trails tie in with those of the BSFNRRA and the Daniel Boone National Forest.

In addition to its geology, Pickett State Park and Forest shares a history with the BSFNRRA, in that much of the land for the preserve was acquired from the Stearns Coal and Lumber Company's holdings. From the early 1900s until the 1960s, the Stearns company operated timber, railroad, and coal operations in and around Fentress and Pickett counties in Tennessee and McCreary County, Kentucky (Perry 1983, 203–14). However, on December 18, 1933, the Stearns firm donated some of its Tennessee holdings (10,050 acres) to the State of Tennessee. These acres became the genesis of the state park and forest, named after the Tennessee county in which the preserve is located. At the time of this writing, the park and forest contained 11,752 acres, but efforts were under way to secure additional acreage through donation.

In the 1930s, Pickett State Park and Forest was the site of a large project of the federal government's Civilian Conservation Corps (CCC), with two CCC camps. During the difficult years of the Depression, many young men both earned a living and acquired valuable work skills through their "Three C" experiences. These young men lived and worked in a paramilitary fashion, with education as part of the daily regimen. Most of their earnings were sent home to families. The men of the CCC produced an extraordinary system of trails and roads which still are in use today in the state park.

The Civilian Conservation Corps was active in several other parks in East Tennessee, particularly nearby Frozen Head State Park near Wartburg, Cumberland Mountain State Park near Crossville, and the Great Smoky Mountains National Park. Anyone who uses our eastern state and national parks for recreation and hiking owes a tremendous debt to the thousands of unrecognized CCC workers of the 1930s. They fashioned a lasting conservation legacy for our nation, and it is appropriate that both Pickett and Frozen Head state parks have been dedicated to their memory.

Tennessee Highway 154 runs through Pickett State Park. Along a 3-mile stretch of this road are located six significant geological features, the farthest from the road being only a little over 0.6 mile. It actually is possible, in a short time, to drive your motor vehicle from one feature to the next, park, and make the short hike to view each one. For those on a more relaxed schedule, there are connector trails which make it possible to visit the Indian Rockhouse near the park's southern entrance, cross the highway to Hazard Cave with its window arch, continue on to Second Chance Arch, and end with one of the finest and most graceful arches in the region, Natural Bridge. This series of features can be enjoyed with a one-way hike of only 0.9 mile. And just up the road from Natural Bridge is Hidden Passage Trail, with a fine column arch six feet tall right on the trail within a half-mile of the trailhead. Just below this unique column arch is Hidden Passage itself, an impressive archway formed from the collapse of a rockshelter, through which passes the trail which bears its name.

The finest natural arch in the state park is the Natural Bridge (sometimes called the "Highway 154 Arch" because of its proximity to that road). Another arch in the state park, called Pickett Lake Natural Bridge, is worth seeing, as is Hazard Cave, with its window arch.

All in all, Pickett State Park is a pleasant surprise. A visit to the Big South Fork area would not be complete without a day, or preferably an overnighter or two, in Pickett park. Pickett State Park has cabins for rent, and a campground. Canoes for paddling on the lake can be rented during the summer. Be sure to stop at the park office when you arrive and pick up the "Pickett Trails" map which shows the color coding and general routes of the several hiking trails in the park. You can write or phone for more information on the state park (see appendix B for the address and phone number).

Indian Rockhouse

Maps: USGS Quad Sharp Place, TN/KY. See map 1 in this guidebook.
Hiking Distance: 0.2 mile, one way.
Directions: From the Bandy Creek Visitor Center, drive 1.5 miles to Tennessee Highway 297 via the paved Bandy Creek Road. Turn right and go west 10.5 miles to the intersection with Tennessee Highway 154 at Sharp Place. Turn right here and go north 2.8 miles to the entrance sign to Pickett State CCC Memorial State Park. Park on the left where the Hazard Cave sign is located. The trail to Indian Rockhouse is directly east across the road and is identified by a trail sign.

Description: This is one of several delightful short hikes along Highway 154 in Pickett State Park. This state park offers the visitor a most accessible connector route to the geological features located along or only a short distance away from Tennessee

Indian Rockhouse. Photograph by David Morris. Used by permission.

Highway 154, which runs through the middle of the park. It is possible to walk to Indian Rockhouse, then cross the road west to Hazard Cave and Window Arch, then proceed north along the trail to Second Chance Arch and on to Natural Bridge—all in the short distance of 0.9 mile one way. In less than a mile, you can observe five unique geological features and in the process have a great day hike (see section on the Indian Rockhouse–Natural Bridge Connector Trail in this guidebook).

Indian Rockhouse Trail starts across Highway 154 from the Hazard Cave Parking Lot; be careful when crossing the highway. This short trail drops down to the large rockshelter, which most likely was used by prehistoric Indians as a shelter site over thousands of years. One of the larger rockshelters in the Big South Fork country, Indian Rockhouse is easily reached.

Rockshelters are geological features created by the weakening of softer sandstone beneath bluffs or waterfalls. Here you see seasonal water dripping from above. In the past, this water erosion weakened less resistant rock, which finally broke off and fell, creating an alcove or recess in the bluff wall. Over time, this and other rockshelters continued to enlarge, as more roof material weakened and fell. This shelter is a classic example of the rock breakdown which creates these natural rockhouses.

This rockshelter contains an actual arch feature, albeit a small one. On the lower east corner of the wall of the rockshelter is a recognizable arch dome, with just a half-inch of space separating it from the bluff wall.

Thousands of rockshelters in the Big South Fork area provided native peoples with a place to get out of the rain and cold. Archaeologists have found the remains of flint or chert tools and weapons and ancient charcoal firepits in rockshelters such as this one. Today, the cultural material that prehistoric Americans left in these rockshelters is protected by law from digging or surface hunting. *Please do not look for artifacts or tools in any of the natural features in the area.*

Retrace your steps back to the Hazard Cave Parking Lot. See the following arch description for directions to Hazard Cave Window Arch. You can also refer to the Indian Rockhouse–Natural Bridge Connector Trail section for another option for seeing several landform features in one hike.

Hazard Cave/Window Arch

Maps: USGS Quad Sharp Place, TN/KY. See map 1 in this guidebook.

Hazard Cave/Window Arch. Photograph by David Morris. Used by permission.

Hiking Distance: 0.25 mile, one way.

Directions: From the Bandy Creek Visitor Center, drive 1.5 miles to Tennessee Highway 297 via the paved Bandy Creek Road. Turn right and drive west 10.5 miles to Sharp Place, where you will intersect Tennessee Highway 154. Turn right here and proceed north 2.8 miles into Pickett State Park. Look for a pullout on the left in front of the sign indicating "Pickett Civilian Conservation Corps Memorial State Park." Park here. This is the beginning point for the short hike to Hazard Cave.

Description: This is an easy hike of a quarter-mile to a large rockshelter with a rare tension dome window arch. The rockshelter is not actually a cave, but merely a large recess in the sandstone wall, giving the appearance of a large limestone cave entrance. The name of this feature sounds intimidating: Hazard Cave. However, its name derives not from any inherent danger, but rather from James O. Hazard, an early employee of Pickett State Forest.

From the Hazard Cave Parking Lot on Highway 154, take the foot trail down thirty-two concrete steps to the base of a bluffline. Follow the trail to the left as it descends gently around the bluffline.

During the wet season, there is active water drainage along the bluffline to your left as you walk on a wooden boardwalk constructed because of the area's moist character. You'll notice wooden fencing on the left along the base of the bluff. This barrier protects a threatened plant species called Lucy Braun Snakeroot (*Eupaterium Luciae Brauniae*), which grows in the shaded confines of sandstone rockshelters like Hazard Cave. It needs the moisture of the seeps and drainages coming off the bluffline. This plant blooms in late summer. Please help protect it by staying off the area behind the wooden fence.

The area along the bluff and at Hazard Cave is as sandy as a Florida beach. The sedimentary rock in the bluff to your left has a stratum of very soft composition Rockcastle Conglomerate sandstone, some of which is so soft that it can be crumbled in your hand. This soft sandstone has eroded off the cliff and off the interior of the Hazard Cave rockshelter to form a very thick "beach" all along the bluffline. On a sunny afternoon in June 1997, on a trip to Hazard Cave, I met some visitors from Florida who asked me seriously how the state park personnel carried in all that sand below the bluff. I thought at first that they were kidding. They weren't. They were truly amazed when I told them the actual origin of the sand.

This "cave" contains a very interesting small feature, a narrow slit tension dome arch at the upper front entrance. This feature sometimes is referred to as the Hazard Cave Window Arch, or Hazard Cave Natural Window. Located right inside another of the distinct geological features of the Big South Fork country, a rockshelter, this arch serves as a double attraction.

The best way to see the window arch is to go as far back into the rockshelter as you can and then turn to look at the upper part of the entrance. You'll see a very narrow slit where a tension dome stratum has sagged from the strata above it, opening up the slit. As mentioned earlier in the section on the formation of natural arches, in any cave or natural arch there is a tension dome which provides support for horizontal strata that are unsupported by underlying rocks. That is how arches and caves remain intact (Corgan and Parks 1979, 9, 11). Without this element, the features would collapse before they ever had a chance to form. The tension dome contains a rock stratum which acts as if it were a beam anchored in the opposite sides of the clearance—like a steel girder running horizontally from one vertical support to another in a building under construction. Gravity and erosion tend to weaken these tension layers, and they can start to sag. When a stratum sags, a slit can open up above it. That is what happened at Hazard Cave. Here we have a large geological feature (the rockshelter) and a very small lintel deck which technically can be described as an arch.

The origin of this small arch, then, is a geological process called "sagging" (Corgan and Parks 1979, 12). Apparently, at least two tension dome systems of rock layers, or strata, support the mouth of the "cave" and the roof. The rocks in the roof of the cave receive more groundwater erosion and as such weather more rapidly than the entrance of the cave. Therefore, differential erosion has caused the beds of sandstone above the cave mouth to sag, leaving a narrow gap between rock layers, forming the window. Some commentators have suggested that the sandstone layer sagging at Hazard Cave may be nearing the point of collapse (Corgan and Parks 1979, 74).

The window arch in Hazard Cave is only 1.5 feet high. The cave entrance is 122 feet wide and 18 feet high.

As you look around, you can see why alcoves like these served as shelters for Indian hunters and gatherers thousands of years ago. In the Big South Fork country, thousands of such rockshelters were used extensively by aboriginal Americans in the Archaic and Woodland cultural periods, as long as ten to twelve thousand years ago. This alcove certainly provides shelter, as you will discover if you visit the site on a rainy day, as I have. Pause a moment to consider not only the geology here, but the prehistoric archaeology also.

When you are ready to leave, you can continue walking north on the Hazard Cave Loop Trail to connect with trails to the Natural Bridge off Highway 154. Or retrace your steps back to your vehicle. For an additional attraction while in the area, after you return to the parking lot, cross Highway 154 to the Indian Rockhouse Trail, a short hike of 0.2 mile one way to another interesting rock overhang shelter.

From Hazard Cave, be sure to visit the Natural Bridge (also called the Highway 154 Arch), a mere 0.5 mile north on the left of Highway 154 where you'll see a picnic table. Also, only 0.3 mile from Natural Bridge is Second Chance Arch, another arch located in Pickett Park within close proximity to others.

It is possible to combine the trails to Indian Rockhouse, Hazard Cave, Second Chance Arch, and Natural Bridge in a single short day hike. All these features are located within a mile of each other. For this hiking option, see the description for the Indian Rockhouse–Natural Bridge Connector Trail.

Natural Bridge (Highway 154 Arch)

Maps: USGS Quad Sharp Place, TN/KY. See map 1 in this guidebook.

Hiking Distance: 40 yards, one way.

Directions: From the Bandy Creek Visitor Center, drive 1.5 miles to Tennessee Highway 297 via the paved Bandy Creek Road. Turn

Natural Bridge. Photograph by David Morris. Used by permission.

right and go west 10.5 miles to the junction with Tennessee Highway 154 at Sharp Place. Turn right here and proceed north 3.3 miles into Pickett State Park to a picnic area on the left. There is a sign here for Natural Bridge. The arch, which is a very short distance to the west, can be seen from the picnic area.

Description: The sign at the picnic area above this arch reads "Natural Bridge," but some people refer to the arch as the "Highway 154 Arch," since it is right off Tennessee Highway 154. Natural Bridge in Pickett Park has a height of 23.5 feet and a span length of 86 feet. It is one of the most accessible arches in the area, being located right off the highway at a convenient picnic area with a table. You don't even have to walk down to the arch. You can see it from the picnic area. There is a stone trail leading down to the arch; be careful when using the trail.

Corgan and Parks, in *Natural Bridges of Tennessee,* describe this arch as having two structurally separate components of cross-bedded sandstone strata (71). In essence, it is a large natural cantilever, with two independent parts touching each other. This does not imply, however, that the arch was formed from such processes as collapse or rockfall or gravity, in which independent rocks change position and align themselves in such a way as to produce an arch or passageway. This arch is one span; it simply has at least two components of cross-bedded strata composing it, a factor that adds to its interest.

This graceful arch was caused by widening of a joint from the main cliff, and by headward erosion. Corgan and Parks suggest that it probably is very old, due to its separation from the main cliff and the thinness of the lintel. They suggest that this arch may be near the point of collapse, although there is no way to ascertain this scientifically without recurrent examination to check for fractures (Corgan and Parks 1979, 71). This underscores the need for the public to stay off arch lintels or decks.

While at Natural Bridge, don't miss the opportunity to see another smaller arch only 0.3 mile to the south. This smaller arch, Second Chance Arch, can be found by following the Natural Bridge Trail to the left of the picnic table on Highway 154 (see description for Second Chance Arch in this guidebook).

A great way to see five different geological features within a distance of 1 mile is to take the Indian Rockhouse–Natural Bridge Connector Trail described in this guidebook. This trail takes you to Natural Bridge, Second Chance Arch, Hazard Cave (with its unique window arch), and Indian Rockhouse. This hike is about 2 miles round trip.

Second Chance Arch

Maps: USGS Quad Sharp Place, TN/KY. See map 1 in this guidebook.
Hiking Distance: 0.3 mile, one way.
Directions: From the Bandy Creek Visitor Center, drive 1.5 miles to Tennessee Highway 297 via the paved Bandy Creek Road. Turn right and proceed west 10.5 miles to the junction with Tennessee Highway 154 at Sharp Place. Turn right and proceed north on Highway 154 for 2.8 miles. At this point you will pass the entrance sign for Pickett State CCC Memorial Park. Continue on for another 0.5 mile to the picnic table on the left at Natural Bridge. Park here. From this picnic area you can look down on Natural Bridge (also called Highway 154 Arch) prior to walking a short 0.3 mile to Second Chance Arch. From the picnic table, take the trail to the left (Natural Bridge Trail) and proceed south along a bluffline for 0.3 mile until the trail makes a turn to the left. Second Chance Arch is on the left. It can be seen better from around the bend in the trail, where its south entrance is located.

Description: This is a neat little bore-hole passageway which looks like a short cave. It is only 0.3 mile from its larger relative, Natural

Second Chance Arch. Photograph by Kevin Kelley. Used by permission.

Bridge, on the same ridgeline. Both are located on the Natural Bridge Trail.

From the picnic table at the Natural Bridge parking area, take the trail (Natural Bridge Trail) to the left, going south. The trail parallels Highway 154. Before leaving the parking area, take a look at Natural Bridge, which is right below the picnic area. You can walk down to Natural Bridge before starting out for Second Chance Arch—there are stone steps down to this impressive arch just to the west of the picnic table. Be careful descending the stone steps.

The Natural Bridge Trail starts out paralleling Highway 154. It follows a bluffline 30 feet above a drainage, so watch your step along the bluff. After only 0.3 mile, the trail makes a sharp left turn. Just before the turn, on your left, is an opening in the sandstone which looks like a cave. You can peer through this small arch passageway; or you can walk around the bend in the trail to the south side, where the other opening stands. At 5 feet, 11 inches high, this south opening clearance is just tall enough to allow most visitors to stand upright. The width here is 14 feet.

This arch is the result of headward erosion, which worked on both sides of the ridge to create a passageway through the very soft sandstone here. The times I visited the arch in May and early June, copious amounts of water were seeping over the whole ridge which houses both this arch and Hazard Cave 0.3 mile farther south.

Interestingly enough, this bore-hole arch, even with its easy access right along the trail, did not have a name attached to it. Park Ranger David Delk at Pickett State Park, and my search of the literature on Tennessee arches, confirmed that it was nameless. Thus, for purposes of this guidebook, Ranger Delk and I named it "Second Chance Arch," since it is so close to Natural Bridge. By hiking only an additional 0.3 mile from Natural Bridge, you can get a "second chance" to see an interesting arch feature.

This small arch is located in a very soft layer of sandstone. The stone beneath and around the arch passageway is demonstrably soft. You can pick up a fragment from the ground and see how easily it crumbles; please don't disturb rock in the arch itself, however. As mentioned earlier, this nice little passageway arch is located on a corridor in Pickett State Park, which allows the visitor to hike from Natural Bridge to Second Chance Arch, Hazard Cave, and then Indian Rockhouse in a 2-mile round trip (see description of Indian Rockhouse–Natural Bridge Connector Trail in this guide).

Pickett Lake Natural Bridge

Maps: USGS Quad Sharp Place, TN/KY. See map 1 in this guidebook.
Hiking Distance: 0.7 mile, one way.
Directions: From the Bandy Creek Visitor Center, drive 1.5 miles on the paved Bandy Creek Road to Tennessee Highway 297. Turn right and drive 10.5 miles to the junction with Tennessee Highway 154 at Sharp Place. Turn right (north) and go approximately 3.4 miles. As you approach the park office, turn left and follow the signs to the lake picnic area. Park at the picnic area. From this location, you have several options for getting to the arch. These are described below.

Description: This arch has been described as an "incised meander," which, in layman's terms, means that it was formed by the meander (twisting course) of Thompson Creek on two sides of a narrow sandstone ridge (the creek was dammed in the 1930s to form Pickett Lake, also known as "Arch Lake"). Knowledgeable authors describe the origin of this natural bridge as follows: "Prior to impoundment of Thompson Creek, the waters moved down a steep gradient and impinged with great force on the south side of the natural bridge. As waters moved farther downstream, they rounded the meander and struck the north side of the bridge. Intense erosion at stream level

Pickett Lake Natural Bridge. Photograph by Kevin Kelley. Used by permission.

on opposite sides of the meander eventually breached the meander neck at the level of the most easily eroded rock. This is the horizon of the modern opening. The stronger beds at higher elevation have yet to collapse and thus form the lintel of the bridge" (Corgan and Parks 1979, 69). In essence, Thompson Creek ultimately eroded a hole through the narrow finger ridge. This opening in the ridge then was enlarged by natural water flow during floods (before Thompson Creek was dammed).

The opening may have been enlarged further by human activity. During the first third of the twentieth century, a narrow-gauge steam railroad carrying timber out of the area passed through the arch (Manning 1990, 65; Corgan and Parks 1979, 69). It is possible that the arch was enlarged to allow the train to pass through it, although evidence of this is anecdotal. Bob Wheeley, a local river outfitter and guide who has a discerning eye for arches, believes that this arch most likely has been altered to some extent. Billy Glen Smith, who was superintendent of Pickett State Park for many years, told me in January 1998 that he had information that the arch had been widened by about a foot and a half on each side by the M. I.

Thompson Lumber Company, a contractor working for the Stearns Coal and Lumber Company. He said that an individual associated with the contractor told him that, in the 1920s, the arch indeed had been widened to accommodate the passage of the narrow-gauge railroad. Smith mentioned (1998, personal communication) that his informant said that only the sides of the arch had been altered, not the lintel. Jim Terry, a retired Pickett park ranger, also told me he had heard that this arch had been slightly altered by the Thompson Lumber Company (1998, personal communication).

The base supports of this arch lintel lack the symmetry of most natural arches. The supports have some irregular edges and angles, not the smooth shape of naturally eroded arches. These edges could have been made in the process of enlarging this opening to accommodate the passage of a narrow-gauge railway. Even if the arch undoubtedly was created through natural processes, it may have been manipulated to some extent by humans at some point in the past. However, there is no definitive evidence to prove that such enlargement occurred.

Given that this arch is natural in origin, it is a unique geological feature. Until recently it was thought to be the only arch in Tennessee caused directly by the erosion of a neck of a deeply incised meander of a large horizontal stream (Corgan and Parks 1979, 16). However, several reliable persons have visited a smaller incised meander on Laurel Fork in the southern part of the BSFNRRA (Bob Wheeley calls this arch "Mystery Arch"). This Laurel Fork arch is not located on or near a trail.

You have several options for viewing Pickett Lake Natural Bridge. In the summer, you can rent a canoe at the state park and float right under the arch on Pickett Lake, also called "Arch Lake" because of the span. This artificial impoundment of Thompson Creek by the Civilian Conservation Corps (CCC) in 1936 created a recreational lake. In the winter, the lake usually is drained, and then you can walk on the mud flats right under the arch (wear some old boots and watch your step). On the north side of the arch is the small CCC dam on Thompson Creek that created Pickett Lake—another example of the historic infrastructure created by this unique program.

In all seasons, you can hike out to the arch and get a view of Pickett Lake Natural Bridge via the trail system. There are several options for hiking. From the park picnic area, the shortest route is to connect with the Island Trail. To reach the Island Trail, don't cross over the swinging bridge. Go east up the road past the pool entrance to the trail sign reading "Island Trail." You'll ascend some stone steps which go up near some cabins. At the top of these steps, turn left and go 100 yards or so to Cabin Numbers 3 and 4. Island Trail can be reached from here. The Island Trail has turquoise or light blue blazes on trees. It is only a half-mile out to Pickett Lake Natural Arch from this starting point. The Island Trail crosses directly over the arch. Please do not attempt to climb down from the natural bridge. The best way to see this arch from beneath is to rent one of the canoes and paddle out under it in the summer.

Another alternative is to take the longer Lake Trail Loop which starts back at the picnic area. The entire loop is 2.5 miles. If you elect this route, you will cross the swinging bridge over the lake and then follow the red blaze of the Lake Trail. Keep following the red blazes for a mile, until you come to the Thompson Creek dam built by the CCC. From here you can get a good view of Pickett Lake Natural Bridge. Be especially careful around the dam area. You can elect to retrace your steps and go back to your vehicle the way you came, or you can continue on the Lake Trail for another mile to join the Island Trail, which will return you to the cabin area. From there you can return to the picnic area and your vehicle.

Be sure to stop by the park office and pick up a copy of the Pickett State Park trail map prior to hiking. Or consult one of the trail guides to the Big South Fork area for descriptions of this and other Pickett Park trails.

Column Arch

Maps: USGS Quad Sharp Place, TN/KY. See map 1 in this guidebook.
Hiking Distance: 0.6 mile, one way.
Directions: From the Bandy Creek Visitor Center, drive 1.5 miles to Highway 297 via the paved Bandy Creek Road. Turn right and go west 10.5 miles to the junction with Tennessee Highway 154 at Sharp Place. Turn right here and go north 2.8 miles to the entrance to Pickett State Park. (For attractions on the way, be sure to see the descriptions for Indian Rockhouse, Hazard Cave, and Natural Bridge in this guidebook.) Continue on past the park office. In 0.3 mile after passing the office, the road will descend down and across Thompson Creek. As you cross the creek, get ready to pull off the road at a small parking area on the right as you start to ascend the hill. There is room here for just a few vehicles. This is the entry place for Hidden Passage Trail. The trail starts at the parking area.

Description: This arch is located on Hidden Passage Trail, a 10-mile loop trail. You don't have to hike the entire trail to see this arch. You only have to hike 0.6 mile one way along a pleasant trail to get to this neat little geological feature. Right next door to Column Arch is Hidden Passage itself, a passageway through a

Column Arch. Photograph by Kevin Kelley. Used by permission.

collapsed rockshelter. If you hike out to the arch and the Hidden Passage and then retrace your steps back to your vehicle, your total mileage will be only about 1.2 miles.

This delightful trail starts out nicely by following Thompson Creek on its north bank, winding along a pine ridge. The creek is thirty feet below you at the start, running through a dense cover of rhododendron and mountain laurel. The tree blaze for this trail is green.

The trail stays on or near the ridge for the first 0.3 mile and then starts to make turns and drops moderately into a moist hemlock and heath draw. At 0.5 mile, you will come to the loop trail junction, where a trail sign points left to the group camp, and right to Hidden Passage. Go right.

In another tenth of a mile, you'll round a bend. There on your left will be a wooden bench recessed into the rock overhang for use by tired hikers. Next to it, and much more impressive, is Column Arch, a six-foot column eroded out of the sandstone overhang. This arch was unnamed on official maps and in the literature. Pickett State Park Ranger David Delk and I have given it the title "Column Arch" for purposes of this guidebook, based upon its appearance.

This arch column is a gnarled post supporting the east end of the overhang where the bench is located. It looks like a chimney rock, only it is still attached to its parent rock. It forms a narrow arch clearance, which you can examine closely. Please be careful not to damage this unique feature as you examine it. Walking around or through it could wear it down. Help conserve it for many others to appreciate.

This is a combination feature, in that the column has an erosion hole in it and is located in a small rockshelter or overhang. Here softer sandstone below the top of the overhang eroded out, leaving the more resistant rock to be carved into weird geological shapes by weathering and erosion. The rock in the column contains minerals, such as iron. These have strengthened it and made it resistant. Look closely at the column. You can clearly see the horizontal iron-reinforced sedimentary strata in the column. Also note the erosion hole through the column.

Just around the bend is Hidden Passage, a rockshelter which partially collapsed, creating a breakdown arch span. This feature is described in the following section.

Hidden Passage

Maps: USGS Quad Sharp Place, TN/KY. See map 1 in this guidebook.
Hiking Distance: 0.6 mile, one way.
Directions: Follow the directions for Column Arch, above.

Description: This short hike out to Column Arch and Hidden Passage allows you to examine two natural features along a very pleasant trail. The first is an interesting six-foot column arch located right on the trail (described in the preceding section), and the other is a collapsed rockshelter which created a dark passageway through an arch along the trail. Both these features are located only a short distance from the trailhead, so it is unnecessary to hike the entire 10-mile Hidden Passage Trail to enjoy them.

Hidden Passage is the result of a partially collapsed overhang or rockshelter. Erosion caused weaker rock to collapse. This created a passageway through which the trail passes. This collapsed rockshelter has formed a breakdown or rockfall arch, in that a span runs between the two supports. It therefore qualifies as a bona fide arch feature. The passageway is approximately 9 feet high (depending on where you measure) and 30 feet wide. Note the extensive rock breakdown littering the passage. This is a clue to the violent origin of this feature.

You can return to the trailhead by retracing your steps. Or, if you are energetic, you can continue on the entire 10-mile Hidden Passage

Hidden Passage. Photograph by Arthur McDade.

Loop and see other features, such as Crystal Falls. Just a few miles northeast of Hidden Passage is Buffalo Arch, in the Daniel Boone National Forest. From Hidden Passage, you can drive north on Tennessee Highway 154 for 4.5 miles to a gravel road on the right (there is a sign right before this gravel road which indicates "Great Meadows" and "Bell Farm" to the right). Turn onto this gravel road; it is marked as Forest Road 562. Go 0.8 miles to the trail sign on the right for Buffalo Arch Trail 634A. Refer to the description of Buffalo Arch in the Daniel Boone National Forest section of this guidebook for directions to the arch from this location.

Indian Rockhouse–Natural Bridge Connector Trail

Maps: USGS Quad Sharp Place, TN/KY. See map 1 in this guidebook.
Hiking Distance: 0.9 mile, one way.
Directions: From the Bandy Creek Visitor Center, drive 1.5 miles via the Bandy Creek Road to Tennessee Highway 297. Turn right and go west 10.5 miles to the intersection with Highway 154 at Sharp Place. Turn right here, and go 2.8 miles to Pickett State

Indian Rockhouse–Natural Bridge Connector Trail. Photograph by David Morris. Used by permission.

Park. Go north an additional 0.3 mile, and look for the picnic table at Natural Bridge on your left. Park here.

Description: This connector route allows the visitor to park at Natural Bridge and hike a 0.9 mile trail (one way) to experience five geological features (Natural Bridge, Second Chance Arch, Hazard Cave and Window Arch, and Indian Rockhouse). You can then retrace your route to return to your vehicle, or walk north from the Indian Rockhouse Trailhead along Highway 154 back to the picnic area at Natural Bridge. If you do this, be careful along the road; walk well off the shoulder on the grass. The trail also can be started at Indian Rockhouse.

Start the connector trail with a visit to Natural Bridge (described above). Take the Natural Bridge Trail, which starts at the south side of the picnic area, 0.3 mile along the bluff to Second Chance Arch (described above). Continue south on this trail for another 0.2 mile to a sign directing you toward Hazard Cave to the left. The trail makes a hard left turn and ascends gently up onto the bluffline. Hike south along the bluffline with mountain laurel on both sides until, after 0.3 mile, you come to another sign pointing left to Highway

154 and right to Hazard Cave. Go right. Hazard Cave is 0.2 mile farther. At Hazard Cave, take time to look for the Window Arch in the upper entrance of the rockshelter (see description of Hazard Cave Window Arch). Return to the Hazard Cave parking lot and cross Highway 154 to find a short 0.2-mile trail to Indian Rockhouse (described above). After exploring the rockhouse, retrace your steps back to Highway 154. You can walk north off the road 0.5 mile to your vehicle at the Natural Bridge picnic table, or you can retrace your hiking route for a total round trip of 2 miles.

This connector trail can be hiked in reverse, obviously, starting from the Hazard Cave parking area rather than from Natural Bridge.

ARCHES AND FEATURES OF DANIEL BOONE NATIONAL FOREST

In the conservation history of the Big South Fork area, a crucial factor has been the preservation and protection of vast acreage on the Northern Cumberland Plateau. There the Daniel Boone National Forest (DBNF) includes over 670,000 acres in twenty-one counties of eastern Kentucky. The forest's southern boundary is the Tennessee state line; the forest also adjoins the Big South Fork National River and Recreation Area (BSFNRRA) and Pickett State Forest. Interestingly, some of the arches and features that now are included in the BSFNRRA used to be part of DBNF. Yahoo Falls is a prominent geological feature which used to be a part of DBNF prior to the establishment of the BSFNRRA.

This guidebook to the geological features of the Big South Fork area does not cover all of the DBNF. Of seven DBNF ranger districts, only the Stearns district and a small part of the Somerset district in the southern part of the forest are included. There are other fine arches and geological features in the upper DBNF (most notably in the Red River Gorge area, where several impressive arches beckon the explorer), but they are not within the area called the Big South Fork.

Today the national forest bears the name of the famous pioneer, Daniel Boone. Originally it had another name, however, one that was geographically appropriate: the Cumberland National Forest. In the early 1900s, resource exploitation (lumbering, mining) throughout the southern mountains had left widespread environmental degradation. This exploitation occurred in many areas of the Southern Appalachian Mountains, from the Great Smoky Mountains to what would become Shenandoah National Park in Virginia. Attendant economic decline was followed by the Great Depression of the 1930s.

In the first third of the twentieth century, a movement began to establish national forests under the U.S. Forest Service in the eastern United States, comparable to those already established in the West. The purpose was watershed and timber protection. An area called the Cumberland Purchase Unit was established on May 17, 1930, to acquire lands for a national forest in the mountains of eastern Kentucky. Since the area had been logged heavily for decades and the Great Depression put a burden on landowners to keep up their tax payments, the government found many willing sellers of land. On February 24, 1937, President Franklin Roosevelt designated an area that included the current DBNF as the Cumberland National Forest (Perry 1983, 230–31). It remained such until April 11, 1966, when civic-minded individuals prevailed upon the U.S. Forest Service to honor the memory of Kentucky's famous adopted son, one "D. Boone."

Interestingly, Boone was not a native of Kentucky. He was born in Pennsylvania, matured on the Carolina frontier, explored Kentucky, and ultimately settled in Missouri, where he died. Convinced that a name change was proper, President Lyndon B. Johnson in 1966 officially rededicated the federal preserve as the Daniel Boone National Forest.

Most of the arches and natural features of the DBNF described in this guidebook are located in the Stearns Ranger District. This district is just over the Tennessee state line in McCreary County, Kentucky. This district contains 113,353 acres. Of the geological features in the DBNF which are treated in this guidebook, only Natural Arch lies outside this ranger district (it is in the Somerset Ranger District to the north, even though it is in McCreary County).

Daniel Boone National Forest contains a surprising number of accessible natural arches. This is due primarily to the high density of Forest Service roads which crisscross the area. This road density reflects the extensive timber harvesting which has occurred in the forest over the years. Such tree cutting requires that gravel roads be constructed into areas of timber sale. Forest Service timber markers, who explored backcountry areas to mark timber for sale, often discovered natural arches in the DBNF. Many natural arches in the area also were documented by Elmer Boggs, a local county agricultural extension agent, who kept a file on these natural features. Robert Stephens of McCreary County, Kentucky, also has documented many of the arches in the Daniel Boone area.

After a Forest Service timber sale has been concluded and the timber cut, the roads usually remain open to the public for recreational use, opening the area for further exploration. Timber sales and road construction are still going on the forest, although at lower levels than in the past. In contrast, timber harvesting is not allowed on National Park Service lands in the adjacent BSFNRRA, so road densities (and hence access by motor vehicles) are lower in the backcountry there. To find new arches in the BSFNRRA, it is necessary to explore blufflines by foot, cross country. Moreover, once an arch is discovered, public access is more difficult in the BSFNRRA than in the national forest.

Fascinating natural features abound in the southern districts of the DBNF, ranging from the large Natural Arch to the small Robber's Roost. Those interested in exploring the more remote features should contact the U.S. Forest Service's Stearns District Ranger Office on U.S. Highway 27 north of Whitley City, Kentucky, during regular working hours, Monday through Friday. Ask to see the file entitled "Arches and Waterfalls." This file contains photographs and descriptions of twenty-four arches in the Stearns district, nine of which are included in this guidebook.

The Forest Service also has put together a *Recreation Guide to the Stearns Ranger District,* which contains photocopied topographical map references showing the approximate locations of some of the arches. Many of these arches are accessible only with difficulty and involve bushwhacking cross-country, however. For a survey of the geological features in other parts of the Daniel Boone National Forest, particularly the Red River Gorge area, consult Preston McGrain's *The Geological Story of Kentucky* or Robert Ruchhoft's *Kentucky's Land of the Arches: The Red River Gorge* (see "Selected References").

Robber's Roost Arch

Maps: USGS Quad Whitley City, KY. See map 3 in this guidebook.
Hiking Distance: 0.1 mile, one way.
Directions: The following directions are from both the Bandy Creek Visitor Center in the Tennessee section of the BSFNRRA and from the Kentucky Visitor Center in Stearns, Kentucky.

From the Bandy Creek Visitor Center, drive 1.5 miles via the paved Bandy Creek Road to Tennessee Highway 297. Turn left and go east approximately 12 miles to U.S. Highway 27 at Oneida, Tennessee. Go north on Highway 27 to the Tennessee-Kentucky state line, a distance of 11.5 miles. From the state line, continue north another 2 miles to intersect with Kentucky Highway 1470 West (be sure to take Kentucky 1470 *West,* not Kentucky 1470 *East,* which is located 0.4 mile farther north). Turn left onto Highway 1470 West.

If you start from the NPS Visitor Center at Stearns, Kentucky, go south 6.1 miles on U.S. Highway 27 to a junction with Kentucky 1470 West on your right. Turn right onto Highway 1470 West.

After turning onto Highway 1470 West, you will cross the

Robber's Roost Arch. Photograph by Arthur McDade.

Norfolk Southern Railroad tracks. Be sure to look for approaching trains; this is an active line, and this crossing has an automatic train gate which descends when trains approach. Cross the railroad tracks and continue west on Highway 1470 west through a residential area for 2 miles. You will pass the Mount Pleasant United Baptist Church on your left. Continue straight ahead on Highway 1470 West.

At 2.7 miles, you'll cross a bridge over Roaring Paunch Creek (there is no creek sign here, but it is the only large creek that you will cross). Continue straight ahead. You'll pass Bill King Road on the right in 0.1 mile after the creek, and then you'll start an ascent up a hill. The road changes from paved asphalt to gravel. Now you are approaching the boundary of the Daniel Boone National Forest and are getting close to the location of Robber's Roost Arch.

At 3.2 miles, you'll see two mailboxes at a gravel road on the right at the top of the hill. Slow down, because Robber's Roost Arch is just ahead on the left, less than one-tenth of a mile away. You can park at the top of the hill just after the two mailboxes, in a pullout on the right. Do not park in the private driveway. Make sure your vehicle is off the road; this gravel road is used.

Immediately in front of you, beyond where Highway 1470 West

makes a right turn, is a hill. Walk toward it and bear slightly to the right. Look for an unmarked trail which ascends sharply up the hill straight ahead of you. Walk carefully up this trail. In 40 feet, you'll come to the east entrance of Robber's Roost Arch, which looks like a small cave entrance in the sandstone ridge. In the summer, you can even feel cool air wafting through the opening.

If you are adventurous, you can crawl 35 feet through the semi-darkness of this opening to the west entrance, which is larger. If crawling is not your thing, walk over the top of the small ridge and bear right and then left to make your way to the west side of this arch. Be careful of your footing as you descend to the west side.

Description: This is a very interesting arch, one well worth the extra trouble required to find it. It really isn't as isolated as it appears, since it is located within a stone's throw of Kentucky Highway 1470 West, only 3.3 miles from U.S. Highway 27. Also, it involves a hike of less than 300 yards to see it, so it certainly is a moderately easy arch to visit.

This arch is different from any of the others in the Daniel Boone National Forest (Stearns District), in that it looks like a small cave. You have to bend down to peer into the east passageway of this arch. If you didn't know better, you would think you were at the entrance to a small limestone cave, not a sandstone arch. But this feature does qualify as a true arch.

Robber's Roost Arch is the product of headward erosion which ate away at both sides of this narrow finger ridge, creating a bore-hole arch. There is water seepage over both entrances in wet seasons. The east entrance (the side near the road) is the size of a small cave entry, while the west end of the passageway has the appearance of a small rockshelter. The east entrance measures 3 feet high and 4 feet wide. The west entrance has a height of 7 feet and a width of 23 feet. The west entrance has several side pockets or rooms.

The probable origin of this arch was water seeping over the west end of the ridge in a small seasonal waterfall. This water descended to an ancestral ledge a short distance below the lip of the falls, where gravity channeled at least a part of the water back against the rock beneath the ridge. Thus erosion carved out a cavelike passageway through soft and weaker sandstone beneath the finger ridge, allowing some of the water to run downstream and out the east end. At the same time, water also eroded the east side of the ridge. Over hundreds of thousands of years, this erosion created a rather narrow passageway beneath the finger ridge and gave the arch an appearance far different from those of many other arches in the area.

There are a couple of explanations for this feature's name. One story is that the arch passageway was near the old Jacksboro Road, or a spur of it. This road ran from Jacksboro, Tennessee, toward Monticello, Kentucky. Reportedly, robbers used it as a hiding place from which to launch assaults upon passersby. Another story is that there was a salt mine in the area, and robbers would steal the salt from people as they passed by.

When you leave Robber's Roost, be very careful as you descend the steep trail back to your vehicle. Several roads can take you to other natural arches on the Kentucky side of the Big South Fork area. In your vehicle, retrace your route back to U.S. Highway 27 and go left for 6.1 miles to the NPS Kentucky Visitor Center (which is the starting point for most of the Kentucky arch destinations in this guidebook).

Alternatively, from the junction of Kentucky Highway 1470 West and U.S. Highway 27, you can go left and proceed approximately 16 miles north to Kentucky Highway 927, which is the turnoff for Natural Arch, the largest arch on the Kentucky side in the Big South Fork area (see description below). On this route, you will also pass Kentucky Highway 700 on your left, which is the turnoff for Yahoo Arch and Markers Arch.

From Robber's Roost, you also can continue west on the gravel road (Highway 1470 West) for 3.8 miles to the Bear Creek Overlook and the trailhead for Split Bow Arch (bear left at the junction with Ross Road). This route will take you past a sign for the BSFNRRA; past the Bear Creek Gauging Station Road; and, 0.2 mile from this road, to the parking lot at the Bear Creek Overlook (the trailhead for Split Bow Arch). From there you can continue on the gravel road to get back to paved Kentucky Highway 742. You'll pass the Split Bow Arch Overlook where you can get a view of the arch, but it is better to walk the short loop trail to Split Bow and back.

After approximately 1.1 mile from Split Bow Overlook, bear right at the junction. Go another 0.4 mile to a stop sign at Ross Road. Bear left on Ross Road, and continue another 2.0 miles on a narrow gravel road, which finally becomes pavement prior to reaching Kentucky Highway 742 (also called Mine 18 Road). From here you can turn left to go to New and Wagon arches, Cracks-in-the-Rock, and Blue Heron. You can get back to Stearns, Kentucky, and U.S. Highway 27 by turning right and following Highway 742 until it intersects with Kentucky Highway 741. Turn left onto 741 and then left again onto Kentucky Highway 1651. In about 1 mile, you will intersect Kentucky Highway 92. From there, bear right onto Highway 92 and head east to the NPS

Kentucky Visitor Center and U.S. Highway 27. This completes an irregular loop for those who want to explore some of the gravel roads in the area. See map 3, p. 97.

Natural Arch

Maps: USGS Quad Nevelsville, KY. See map 4 in this guidebook.
Hiking Distance: 1 mile, one way.
Directions: From the NPS Visitor Center in Stearns, Kentucky, go east to the traffic light at U.S. Highway 27. Turn left, and go north for approximately 9.5 miles to Kentucky Highway 927 on the left. There is a U.S. Forest Service sign for Natural Arch here. Turn left onto Highway 927, and go 1.7 miles to the Natural Arch picnic area on the right. Go to the end of the picnic area parking lot. If the gate is locked at the entrance, you can park your vehicle (don't block the gate) and walk into the picnic area.

Description: This is the largest natural arch in the Somerset and Stearns ranger districts of the Daniel Boone National Forest. If the term "natural bridge" ever was appropriate for an arch, this is the case. It is surprising that it was not officially named that; perhaps the Forest Service wanted to avoid duplicating the name of another Natural Bridge in another ranger district of the DBNF. Especially

Natural Arch.
Photograph by
Arthur McDade.

from the overlook near the Natural Arch Scenic Area picnic site, however, this feature very closely resembles a bridge. You look across a gulf of trees stretching out below you to an attractive arch deck with an imposing, thick arch lintel a half-mile away. This view from the overlook at the picnic area is one of the most striking in the Big South Fork area.

This beautiful major arch offers the visitor the chance to hike to the arch itself or to take a short walk to the excellent overlook. The starting point is the Natural Arch Scenic Area off Kentucky Highway 927, which has a day-use picnic area. This picnic and recreation area was constructed in the late 1960s by trainees at the U.S. Forest Service Job Corps Center in Pine Knot, Kentucky, not far away. The Natural Arch Scenic Area consists of 945 acres in the headwaters of Cooper Creek, set aside in 1961. In addition to the 1-mile trail to Natural Arch (Forest Service Trail No. 510), there is a 5.1-mile loop trail, called the Buffalo Canyon Trail (Forest Service Trail No. 508). An expansive view of the area also can be had at the Panoramic View Trailhead (Trail No. 528) off Highway 927, 1.5 miles west beyond the picnic area.

Starting at the northern end of the picnic area parking lot, a paved trail (No. 510) leads right to the arch and left to the Natural Arch overlook. The trail to the overlook to the left is only 0.2 mile away and is generally level. The overlook offers an outstanding view of this arch with minimal physical effort. The trail to the right involves a 1-mile hike to get the base of the arch, with some stairs and drop and gain in elevation. There are two overlooks on this arch trail (No. 510), but they are not as good as the overlook on the left prong. Follow the signs for Natural Arch on Trail No. 510 past the junction with the Buffalo Canyon Trail to the arch. At the base of the arch is an interpretive board describing the rock feature.

Natural Arch has a height of 60 feet and a width of 100 feet. It is on U.S. Forest Service property and is part of the DBNF. Natural Arch is another good example of headward erosion: the softer sandstone has been carved out beneath a finger ridge, leaving the more resistant sandstone to form the arch lintel. It is a beautiful arch.

You can return to the picnic area and your vehicle by retracing your steps. After your hike, the picnic area is a nice place to grab a sandwich and enjoy the day.

Natural Arch is easily accessible; a paved path goes all the way to it. Some other interesting trails cover 9 miles in the Natural Arch Scenic Area. For a free pamphlet on the area, entitled "Natural Arch Scenic Area," write to the Daniel Boone National Forest, Stearns District (see appendix B for the address).

Yahoo Arch

Maps: USGS Quad Nevelsville, KY. See map 4 in this guidebook.
Hiking Distance: 1 mile, one way.
Directions: From the NPS Visitor Center at Stearns, Kentucky, turn left on Kentucky Highway 92 and proceed to the intersection with U.S. Highway 27. Turn left and go north approximately 3.4 miles. Turn left at the junction of U.S. Highway 27 and Kentucky Highway 700. There is no sign here for Yahoo Arch; the best indicator is the Whitley City Motel on the right side of Highway 27 at this intersection. Proceed west on Highway 700 across the railroad tracks. Watch for trains—this is an active line of the Norfolk Southern Railway. Continue straight on Highway 700 after the stop sign. At 2.2 miles after turning off U.S. Highway 27, you'll pass a sign for the Daniel Boone National Forest. Continue on for another 0.6 mile.

Be on the lookout for a pullout with a berm on the right. This is the trailhead for Yahoo Arch Trail No. 602. Parking here is limited to only one or two vehicles. If the pullout is full, there is a Forest Service road (Forest Road 6003) on the left a short distance west where you can park. Please don't block the road. At

Yahoo Arch. Photograph by Arthur McDade.

the Yahoo Arch pullout, there is a trailhead sign reading "Yahoo Arch Trail No. 602, Yahoo Arch 1 Mile." This route is the easiest access to Yahoo Arch, 1 mile straight ahead, and it is also the trailhead for Markers Arch 0.5 mile to the right (see description in this guidebook).

For another access to Yahoo Arch with a guaranteed parking space, and for an enjoyable side trip to Yahoo Falls, continue west on Kentucky Highway 700 for an additional mile to the turnoff to the Yahoo Falls picnic area. There is a large NPS sign here pointing right to Yahoo Falls Scenic Area. Turn right here and proceed 1.5 miles on a gravel road to the end of the picnic area parking lot. The trails in the area start at the bulletin board near the restroom facilities. From this location, you have two options to get to Yahoo Arch:

Option 1. Stay on the topside trail 1.3 miles east to Yahoo Arch (do not descend to Yahoo Falls). After about 0.5 mile, you'll come to a signpost showing Yahoo Arch 0.8 mile ahead. Follow this trail to the arch. Look for white diamond blazes on the trees as the trail passes from the BSFNRRA to the Daniel Boone National Forest.

Option 2. This option combines the natural beauty and archaeological interest of Yahoo Falls (at 113 feet, the tallest waterfall in Kentucky and an ancient Native American rockshelter) with the experience of seeing Yahoo Arch. This option is more strenuous— you have to descend more than one hundred steps down to Yahoo Falls and then hike back up to the bluff; but if you're in shape, it is well worth it.

From the bulletin board at the Yahoo Falls parking lot, follow the signs to Yahoo Falls, a quarter-mile to the east (yellow and green arrowhead symbols will be on trees on this trail). Upon reaching Yahoo Falls, follow the trail through the rockshelter. Continue on trail and bear right at the next junction with a connector trail. Continue to bear right as you ascend on the Yahoo Falls Loop. This trail will take you right above the waterfall and the rockshelter. You'll cross Yahoo Creek above the falls. Be careful; watch your step, and stay well back from the lip of the falls. Soon you will intersect with the topside trail (Option 1). A signpost points left for Yahoo Arch, 0.8 mile away. Follow the white diamond blazes to the arch.

Description: Yahoo Arch is an attractive arch located in a moist drainage shrouded in hemlock and rhododendron. It is only 1 mile from Kentucky Highway 700, and 1.5 miles from another interesting arch, Markers Arch (described elsewhere in this guidebook). Additionally, Yahoo Arch is located only 1 mile from

Yahoo Falls, the tallest (113 feet) waterfall in Kentucky. Yahoo Arch's accessibility to Markers Arch and Yahoo Falls makes it a most rewarding day-hike destination. On summer days, the cool vegetation and the shade of Yahoo Arch provide welcome relief after hiking to other features in this area.

Yahoo Arch is a collapsed rockshelter. The rear of an exposed rockshelter—a feature common in the area—collapsed due to erosion. There is breakdown material here to suggest that origin. The collapse left a resistant span of harder sandstone at the front. Once the lintel was created by the collapse of the rear of the rockshelter, erosion kept up the work of rounding the edges and sculpting the arch. This arch has a clearance height of 17 feet, and a span width of 70 feet, 6 inches (DBNF measurements).

There are actually two arches at Yahoo Arch. In addition to the major span, there is a "window arch" four feet high on the east base of the main arch, forming an unusual arch within an arch (a similar phenomenon is visible at nearby Markers Arch). Yahoo may not be the highest of the several natural arches in the Big South Fork area, but it is a beautiful and shady rock feature along an impressive wall of sandstone.

Located on the boundary between the BSFNRRA and the DBNF, Yahoo Arch is situated in a region of the Big South Fork country that is rich in interesting archaeological and botanical features. Not far to the west is the main gorge of the Big South Fork of the Cumberland River. One mile northwest, and connected by a trail, is Yahoo Falls, the highest waterfall in Kentucky. You can combine a trip to Yahoo Arch with a side trip to Yahoo Falls for a wonderful half-day hike, while also seeing Markers Arch (which is a mile and a half south of Yahoo Arch). All these features are worth seeing.

At Yahoo Falls, in an alcove behind the falls, you will find one of the largest rockshelters (also called rockhouses) in the Big South Fork area. This rockshelter was used by ancient people as long as ten thousand years ago. Indians of the Paleo, Archaic, and Woodland cultural periods used this fascinating rockshelter as a temporary shelter, most likely during hunting expeditions into the area. They left behind the record of their passing in the chert and flint points, scrapers, and pottery sherds which have been found here. A National Park Service wayside exhibit on the prehistory of the area is located at the rockshelter, near the base of the falls.

Other rockshelters exist at Yahoo Arch, too. In fact, there is a rockshelter above the arch. This gives a definite clue to the geological origin of this natural arch. As mentioned above, Yahoo Arch itself is the result of a collapsed rockshelter. There is another large rockshelter, just a stone's throw to the north of Yahoo Arch along the trail.

In addition to visiting nearby Markers Arch and Yahoo Falls, while in the area you might want to consider hiking part of the Sheltowee Trace, which runs north and south near Yahoo Falls. This national recreation trail travels 254 miles through Daniel Boone National Forest, Cumberland Falls State Park, Big South Fork National River and Recreation Area, and Pickett State Park. Its name means "Big Turtle," the nickname given to Daniel Boone by the Shawnees. Boone for a time was a captive of the Indians. The Sheltowee Trace traverses approximately 45 miles of the Big South Fork region. It is described in the several trail guides to the area.

Please do not climb on the arch decks, waterfalls, or rock shelters in the area, due to personal safety and natural preservation concerns.

Markers Arch

Maps: USGS Quad Nevelsville, KY. See map 4 in this guidebook.
Hiking Distance: 0.5 mile, one way.
Directions: From the NPS Visitor Center at Stearns, Kentucky, take a left onto Kentucky Highway 92, and drive east 300 yards to U.S. Highway 27. Turn left on U.S. 27 and proceed north 3.4 miles to Kentucky Highway 700 at Marshes Siding. There is no sign at this junction (look for the Whitley City Motel on the right). Turn left onto Kentucky Highway 700. Follow Highway 700 across the railroad tracks (watch for trains—this is an active line), and continue west on Highway 700 after the stop sign. At 2.2 miles after turning off U.S. 27, you'll see a sign for the Daniel Boone National Forest. Continue on for another 0.6 mile and look for a small pullout with a berm on the right. There is a trail sign here designating Yahoo Arch Trail No. 602. Parking is limited. If it is full, more space is available on a gravel Forest Service road (Forest Road 6003) on the left only a short distance west on Highway 700. Make sure you don't block the road, however.

This is the trailhead for both Markers Arch and Yahoo Arch. Just behind the Yahoo Falls Trailhead, a sign directs you right one-half mile to Markers Arch on Forest Service Trail No. 603. The trail to Markers Arch is a dead-end trail to the arch, with no connections. You will have to retrace your steps one-half mile to the junction with the Yahoo Arch Trail (Forest Service Trail No. 602) to return to your vehicle or to continue on to Yahoo Arch.

Description: The Markers Arch Trail follows a level ridge marked with white diamond blazes on trees for the first 0.3 mile before descending through a laurel and rhododendron draw to Markers Arch. The arch is modest in size, 12 feet tall and 25 feet wide. It

Markers Arch. Photograph by Arthur McDade.

exemplifies collapse of a rockshelter and headward erosion. The top of a rockshelter was eroded by water, causing the collapse of the rear end of the shelter and leaving a bridge lintel.

Just as at Yahoo Arch, the eastern base of Markers contains a window arch. This window, two feet high, forms an arch within an arch, a very interesting feature.

Markers Arch is in a little-used part of the Big South Fork area, and only a short, pleasant walk is required to view it. It is located in a moist draw where rhododendron and hemlock provide cooling shade on hot days. Its proximity to Yahoo Arch, Yahoo Falls, and the Sheltowee Trace makes this a wonderful natural area for outings.

While here, if you have the time and energy, visit nearby Yahoo Arch (see description in this guidebook).

Koger Arch

Maps: USGS Quad Barthell, KY. See map 5 in this guidebook.
Hiking Distance: 0.25 mile, one way.
Directions: From the NPS Visitor Center at Stearns, Kentucky, turn right and proceed west on Kentucky Highway 92 for 6.2

miles to Yamacraw Bridge. Cross the Big South Fork of the Cumberland River at Yamacraw. Immediately turn to the left on the west side of the bridge onto Kentucky Highway 1363. Travel 2.0 miles and turn left at the concrete bridge over Rock Creek (there is a sign here indicating Bald Knob and Wilson Ridge to the left). Proceed straight on gravel road 582 (known locally as the Bald Knob or Beech Grove Road) for 0.8 mile. Look carefully on the left for a wooden signpost reading "Koger Arch." The sign is down in a creek drainage and can be covered with vegetation in warm weather. There is limited parking along the road in front of the sign. Follow the Koger Arch Trail (Daniel Boone National Forest Trail No. 633) one-quarter mile to the arch.

Description: This arch is located off a little-traveled gravel road in a quiet part of the Big South Fork country. You aren't likely to find many people in the area. From the parking area, descend across a seasonal creek up to signboards directing you left on Forest Service Trail No. 633. This trail turns left, paralleling Bald Knob Road, and ascends gently for a short distance up Coon Patch Ridge to Koger Arch. This arch was formed from the erosion and

Koger Arch. Photograph by Arthur McDade.

collapese of the back part of a rockshelter. This arch once was a
rockshelter, an alcove in the side of a hill. Something—most likely
water seeping through a joint crack—caused the back of the
ancestral rockshelter to cave in, leaving the front part of the
rockshelter as an arch lintel.

This history is clearly visible when you get to the arch. Walk
under the arch and up through the widened crack or joint which
separates the arch from the ridge. Here you can see the breakdown
rock that caved in at the back of the alcove. Try to imagine when
the space between the ridge and the arch span was only a small
crack, before the collapse. Koger Arch has a height of 18 feet and
a width of 91 feet (DBNF measurements).

Of additional interest in the area are the abandoned railroad
bridge at Yamacraw, and the old Kentucky and Tennessee (K&T)
Railway grade along Kentucky Highway 1363. You passed these
earlier and will pass them again as you exit back to Kentucky
Highway 92. Yamacraw was a mining area of the Stearns Coal
and Lumber Company, and the K&T was the company's railroad
line. The original span of the abandoned Yamacraw railroad
bridge still stands guard over the Big South Fork of the
Cumberland River. This bridge is private property; do not cross
it. For more information on the Stearns Coal and Lumber
Company's operations in the area, visit the Blue Heron
Community in the BSFNRRA, and the Stearns–McCreary County
Museum in Stearns, Kentucky.

You can return to Kentucky Highway 1363 by retracing your
driving route from Koger Arch. At the junction with KY 1363,
you can turn right to return to Kentucky Highway 92 to Stearns,
Kentucky; or you can turn left and proceed to several other arches
(for Hickory Knob Arch, Gobbler's Arch, and Hollow Rock Arch,
see guidebook descriptions and arch location map).

Hickory Knob Arch

Maps: USGS Quad Bell Farm, KY. See map 5 in this guidebook.
Hiking Distance: 10 yards, one way.
Directions: From the NPS Visitor Center at Stearns, Kentucky,
take Kentucky Highway 92 west for 6.2 miles to the Yamacraw
Bridge over the Big South Fork of the Cumberland River. After
crossing the bridge, turn left onto Kentucky Highway 1363 and
go approximately 10 miles to Hickory Knob Church Road on
the left. Turn left onto this gravel road and proceed 2 miles, at
which point the road makes an ascent. Hickory Knob Arch will
be on the left as the road bears to the left near the top of the

Hickory Knob Arch. Photograph by Arthur McDade.

gentle ascent. The gravel road actually crosses the lintel of the arch. You can pull off the road to the right of the arch or park farther south. Please do not block the road; look for a pullout space and walk back to the arch.

Description: This is undoubtedly the easiest natural arch to find in all of the Big South Fork country. It lies close to a gravel road; in fact, the gravel road goes right over it! In the winter, when the surrounding vegetation is down, you can actually see the arch from your vehicle as you approach it.

This arch is the result of the collapse of a rockshelter. When you walk down through this arch from the north, you can see a bluffline on the south of the road ridge containing many pocket rockshelters. The whole ridge along which the gravel road travels has rockshelters on its south side.

Looking up at the lintel of Hickory Knob Arch, you can see a crack in the arch span running north and south. Even today, water seeps through this crack during wet seasons. Over thousands of years, this seepage probably weakened the roof of this particular rockshelter. The resulting collapse of the rear portion of the rockshelter's roof left a span at the entrance, giving us the arch we see today. There is breakdown material beneath the arch lintel—a telltale clue to the probable origin of this natural arch. The arch also has the asymmetry associated with arches caused by cataclysmic events such as the collapse of a rockshelter.

This arch measures 16 feet high and 24 feet wide, according to Bill Brumm of the Daniel Boone National Forest.

Return 2 miles back the way you came, to Kentucky Highway 1363. From this highway, turn right to return to Kentucky Highway 92 to Stearns, Kentucky (the way you came); or, by turning left, proceed a short distance to the nearby road junction at Bell Farm for options to several other arches in the area (see descriptions of Gobbler's Arch and Hollow Rock Arch which follow).

Gobbler's Arch

Maps: USGS Quad Bell Farm, KY. See map 5 in this guidebook.
Hiking Distance: 0.7 mile, one way.
Directions: From the NPS Visitor Center in Stearns, Kentucky, turn right on Kentucky Highway 92 and proceed west 6.2 miles to Yamacraw Bridge. Cross the bridge and turn left on Kentucky Highway 1363. Continue on Kentucky 1363 for 11 miles to Bell Farm, where there is a stop sign. Turn left here on the gravel road (Road 139). Go past the entrance to the Bell Farm Horse Camp and ascend the gravel road 4.5 miles to Peter's Mountain, where you will see a National Park Service sign and a trailhead parking area. Turn right here onto Divide Road and go 0.5 mile to a dirt road on the right (Forest Service Road 6105). Turn right on this road. Check the road conditions as you go. This road can be muddy and can have tree debris blown down in storms. Drive or walk 0.55 mile on this road to the Mark Branch Loop Trailhead and then an additional 0.2 mile until the roadway becomes a four-wheel track. (If road conditions become inappropriate for your vehicle prior to arriving at this location, park on the side of the road near the Mark Branch Loop Trail sign and walk along the gravel road north to where the trail enters the woods.)

At this point, it will appear that the road has vanished into the woods, becoming an obscure single-track Jeep track. Park and hike along the Jeep track for 0.3 mile until you come to the trail sign for Gobbler's Arch Trail on the left. Take this trail 0.2 mile to the arch.

Description: This is a pleasant, easy day hike after you negotiate the road to the trailhead. Getting to the trailhead along Forest Road 6105 during wet months is the only part of the excursion

Gobbler's Arch. Photograph by Arthur McDade.

which might be difficult to accomplish in a street vehicle. As mentioned, you may park your vehicle on gravel near the Mark Branch Loop Trailhead and walk approximately 0.5 mile along a Jeep trail (which is FR 6105) to the Gobbler's Arch Trailhead. (This Jeep trail can be overgrown in the summer.) After arriving at the trailhead, you'll see a Forest Service sign for the Gobbler's Arch Trail, showing the arch 0.2 mile away. Terminal destinations are shown for Hemlock Grove and a junction with the Sheltowee Trace. From the trailhead sign, hike on the Gobbler's Arch Trail through a cool forest of Virginia pine, mixed hardwoods, and laurel, along a soft pine-needle path.

As you approach the arch, you will come to a Forest Service sign reading "Gobbler's Arch." The trail goes left here, down some log water bars across the trail. (On my most recent visit, these log water-bar steps had been chewed up by horse use over them, and a large tree had fallen across the trail.) The arch is a short distance beyond, to the right.

Gobbler's Arch is 11 feet, 9 inches high and 50 feet in its base width. It was created by the collapse of a rockshelter. In fact, today, as you approach it, it appears to be merely a rockshelter beneath a sandstone ridge, one of many thousands in the Big South Fork area. You cannot tell that it has an arch span until you are close to it.

After visiting this arch, you can return to your vehicle by retracing your steps and driving back out Forest Service Road 6105 to its junction with Divide Road. Turn left on Divide Road and go 0.5 mile to Peter's Mountain; then turn left and descend Forest Road 139 to Bell Farm and the junction with paved Kentucky Highway 1363. At this junction with Highway 1363, you can turn left and continue on gravel Road 564 toward Hollow Rock Arch (see description of this arch below), or you can turn right and reverse your route back to Stearns, KY.

The Gobbler's Arch Trail is a 2.2-mile connector with the Sheltowee Trace National Recreation Trail and the Mark Branch Trail in the DBNF. Check the hiking guides for the Big South Fork area for connections to the Sheltowee Trace and other trails in the area.

Hollow Rock Arch

Maps: USGS Quad Bell Farm, KY. See map 5 in this guidebook.
Hiking Distance: 0.2 mile, one way.
Directions: From the NPS Visitor Center at Stearns, Kentucky, turn right on Kentucky Highway 92 and go west for 6.2 miles to Yamacraw Bridge. Cross over the Big South Fork of the Cumberland River at Yamacraw, and turn left onto Kentucky Highway 1363 immediately, on the west side of the bridge. Proceed on Highway 1363 for 11 miles to Bell Farm. You'll come to a stop sign here. Turn right onto the gravel road marked 564 (Parkers Mountain Road). Go straight on this road for 1.2 miles until you reach a junction with Road 137. Here, stay on 564 by bearing right, and start a meandering ascent. A mile from the junction with 137, you'll reach the top of the grade, and an unmarked gravel logging road will be on your right. This road leads 0.2 miles to Hollow Rock Arch on the left. Since this gravel road can be rough and turning around to come out can be difficult, don't take it. Park your vehicle on the shoulder of 564 (be sure to park totally off the roadway) and walk the short distance to the arch. As of this writing, there is logging activity a short distance down the gravel road, so be on the lookout for logging trucks.

Description: Hollow Rock Arch is a classic finger ridge arch. This arch was created by headward erosion working on both sides of the solitary finger ridge, forming a medium-sized arch at the base of the long ridge. During the winter, you can actually see the hole

*Hollow Rock
Arch. Photograph
by Arthur
McDade.*

in the ridge from a hundred feet below, as you approach on Road
564. Look up carefully through the trees on the hillside on the right
as you ascend after the junction with Road 137 (Parkers Mountain
Road). It is impressive to see the long ridge through the barren
winter trees with a breeze hole right through its base. Hence the
name "Hollow Rock."

The arch is a medium-sized one. It is supporting a whole ridge
line. It is 8 feet high in clearance height and 63 feet wide at its base
(DBNF measurements). Stand in the middle of this arch and look
both south and north through the arch hole to see both sides of
the ridge. Think of the immense weight of the entire ridge on top
of the arch, with you right under it. You can appreciate the natural
geometry of arch construction at a place like this.

When you look south through the trees, you are looking at the
drainage of Rock Creek, with Peter's Mountain farther south. The
best view is had in the winter, as is the case generally for all the
arches, since lush vegetation obscures the vista in other seasons.
Were it not for occasional timber harvesting in the general area,
it would be an idyllic scene. Even so, this is a remarkable arch.

Buffalo Arch

Maps: USGS Quad Sharp Place, TN/KY. See map 5 in this guidebook.
Hiking Distance: 0.7 mile, one way.
Directions: The directions to this arch start from the National Park Service's Bandy Creek Visitor Center rather than from its Kentucky Visitor Center, because this route entails considerably less travel by gravel road and also will allow one to visit the Pickett State Park arches en route.

From the Bandy Creek Visitor Center, drive 1.5 miles on the paved Bandy Creek Road to Tennessee Highway 297. Turn right and go west 10.5 miles to Tennessee Highway 154 at Sharp Place. Go right (north) into Pickett State Park and Forest. While passing through Pickett, you can visit several landforms within close proximity to Highway 154 if you have the time and energy (see the descriptions for Pickett State Park in this guidebook).

Continue past the sign indicating Pickett State CCC Memorial Park. You will pass the pullout for Hazard Cave and a picnic table on the left, where you can see Natural Bridge. After passing the park office on your left, proceed 5.1 miles north on Tennessee High-

Buffalo Arch. Photograph by Kevin Kelley. Used by permission.

way 154 to the Kentucky state line, where the name of the highway changes to Kentucky Highway 167. As of this writing, there is no state line marker showing the change of state or highway number.

Continue north on the same road after the state line, and go 0.3 miles to a gravel road (Forest Road 562) on your right. There is a sign on Highway 167 indicating Great Meadows and Bell Farm to the right. Turn right. As you make the right turn, you'll see another sign for "Daniel Boone National Forest." Drive east on this gravel road 0.8 miles to a dirt road on your right. There is a wooden sign here for the Parkers Mountain (Trail No. 634) and Buffalo Arch trailheads (Trail No. 634A). The sign shows the distance to the Buffalo Arch Trailhead as 0.4 mile. Turn right onto this dirt road and park at the side of the road.

From here on, the road is not recommended for street vehicles. This road can have mudholes, especially in wet weather, so four-wheel drive is recommended if you want to drive in. If you do not have four-wheel drive, just park your vehicle at the entrance to this Jeep road and walk the rest of the way in. On foot, it is only approximately 0.7 mile to Buffalo Arch from the beginning of the dirt road. Park your vehicle there and walk the road for 0.1 mile, until you see a white arrow on a brown background pointing you to the right. (There is another Jeep road bearing left. Go right.) Continue hiking down the sandy road for 0.3 mile, until you come to the Parkers Mountain Trailhead on the left. Continue past this trailhead along a Jeep road for 0.2 mile, until you see an arrow pointing right toward Buffalo Arch Trail. Follow the white diamond shapes on the trees to the right. The arch is only 0.2 mile along this trail.

Description: This arch is a bit more isolated than most, and it is not as large as Natural Arch, but it is well worth a visit. If you park at the entrance to the Jeep road and walk in, the round trip is only about 1.4 miles. This trail is a great day hike, passing through a pleasant hardwood forest near the Tennessee-Kentucky state line before gently bending around and arriving at Buffalo Arch.

The first thing that strikes you, upon approaching Buffalo Arch, is its location at the end of a sandstone ridge. The arch is actually the grounding of the south-north ridge, a sort of "flying buttress." This arch is a thing of beauty. Its parent ridge tapers gracefully, culminating in the large arch lintel at the north end. There are other ridgeline arches in the Big South Fork area, but none seems as crucial to the structural integrity of its parent ridge as Buffalo. One can imagine that Buffalo Arch's lintel is a gnarled finger grasping frantically, trying to keep the ridgeline from slipping farther south into Tennessee.

Buffalo Arch was formed by headward erosion which ate away this ridge end. The arch has a deep sandy floor, the remains of soft sandstone which has been eroded from beneath the arch lintel. The feature lacks the rock breakdown found beneath some arches. Consequently, it invites the visitor to sit down or to amble around, looking at its impressive span from a variety of angles. The arch is moderately large; a Daniel Boone National Forest file titled "Arches and Waterfalls" assigns it a clearance height of 18 feet, 6 inches, and a span width of 81 feet, 8 inches.

A trail guide to the Daniel Boone National Forest relates one account of how the arch got its name: Indians used it to hunt woodland buffalo from an elevated location. Perhaps this is true; deer hunters today employ tree stands for a similar purpose.

Buffalo Arch has a charming location in an undeveloped, quiet part of the Big South Fork country. Away from paved roads and not far north of the interesting natural features in nearby Pickett State Park, just south in Tennessee, this site is seldom, if ever, crowded. In my twenty-odd trips to Buffalo, I have not seen many persons other than my own party. If you are looking for graceful symmetry, geological beauty, and solitude, then Buffalo Arch is highly recommended.

POSTSCRIPT

This guidebook represents four years of fieldwork and over one thousand miles of motor vehicle travel. I visited all the geological features included here at least three times, and most I visited many times more. I measured arches and other features located off busy paved highways and solitary backcountry trails. The weather ranged from dead of winter to heat of summer, from sunny and warm to wet and cold. I learned by hard experience that the best time to see these features (and accomplish the field research) was in winter cold, when the vegetation cover was gone and the copperheads, rattlesnakes, yellow jackets, and ticks were sleeping soundly in the forest carpet below.

I remember a June day in Pickett State Park on the Hidden Passage Trail. A late afternoon thunderstorm, accompanied by lightning, pummeled me. I hiked hurriedly along the trail in water up to my ankles, trying to get back to my vehicle at the trailhead. The hemlock trees, mountain laurel, and rhododendron, all heavy with rain, drooped dark limbs over the trail as if to block any remaining light. Just as I passed through Hidden Passage and the gnarled finger of Column Arch, the bottom fell out of the sky, drenching me thoroughly. Together, the hovering vegetation and dark geological features cast a mysterious gloom over the trail. As thunder booms and lightning cracks came all too close for comfort, I thought that, hunched over in my hooded rain parka and speeding along in the rain in a deep, dark forest, I must look like an elf or a Hobbit out of J. R. R. Tolkien's Lord of the Rings. Even though the day had turned wet and gloomy, I was happy to have documented several arch features.

That day was indicative of the deep satisfaction provided by this whole project—that even in less than desirable conditions I still could find a sense of magic and wonder in these hills.

APPENDIX A: MAPS

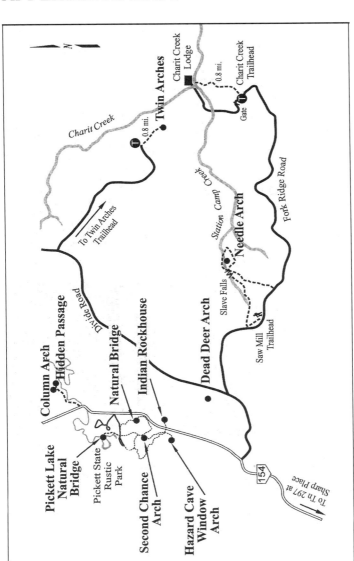

Map 1. Twin Arches, Needle Arch, and Pickett State Park Arches.

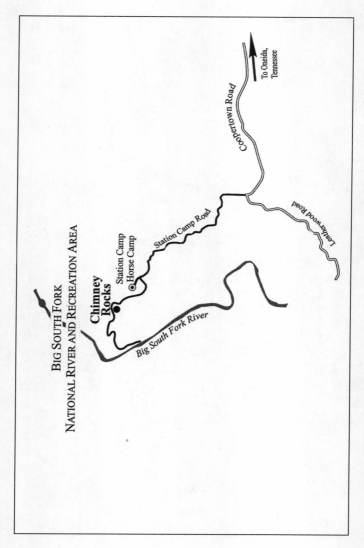

Map 2. Chimney Rocks, Station Camp.

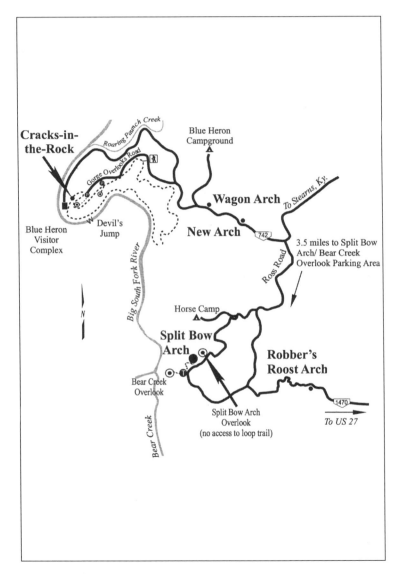

Map 3. Split Bow Arch, New Arch, Wagon Arch, Cracks-in-the-Rock, and Robber's Roost Arch.

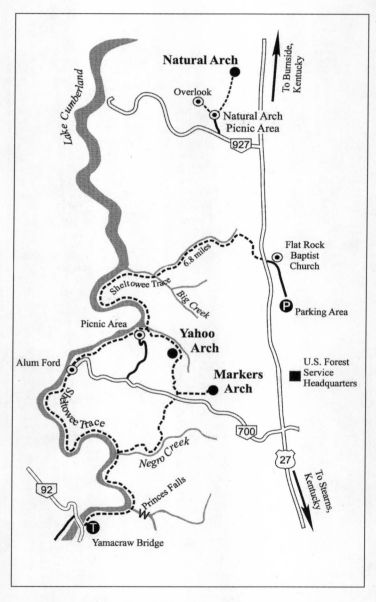

Map 4. Yahoo Arch, Markers Arch, and Natural Arch.

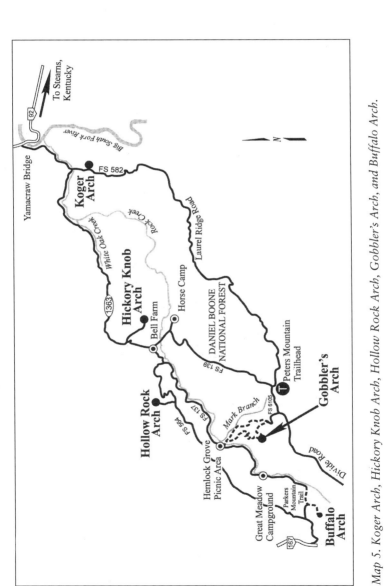

Map 5. Koger Arch, Hickory Knob Arch, Hollow Rock Arch, Gobbler's Arch, and Buffalo Arch.

APPENDIX B: ADDRESSES AND TELEPHONE NUMBERS

State and Federal Agencies

Big South Fork National River and Recreation Area
4564 Leatherwood Road
Oneida TN 37841
Park Headquarters (423) 569-9778
Bandy Creek Visitor Center (931) 879-3625
Kentucky Visitor Center (606) 376-5073
Blue Heron (606) 376-3787

Daniel Boone National Forest (606) 376-5302
Stearns Ranger District (606) 376-5323
        P.O. Box 429
        Whitley City KY 42653

Pickett State Park
        (931) 879-5821
        Rock Creek Route, Box 174
        Jamestown TN 38556

Concessionaires

Big South Fork Scenic Railway
        (800) 462-5664 or (606) 376-5330
        P.O. Box 368
        Stearns KY 42647

Charit Creek Lodge
        (423) 429-5704
        250 Apple Valley Road
        Sevierville TN 37862

Eastern National Park and Monument Association
        (931) 879-3625
        c/o Big South Fork NRRA
        4564 Leatherwood Road
        Oneida TN 37841

GLOSSARY

Appalachian Plateaus Province An elevated sedimentary upland stretching from Alabama north to Pennsylvania.

Anticline A geologic feature in which strata are bent in an upfold.

Arch Landform span formed by weathering and erosion.

Chert A dense, hard sedimentary rock or mineral composed of submicrocrystalline quartz. Unless colored by impurities, chert is white, in contrast to flint, which is dark or black.

Clastic Texture Texture that characterizes a rock made up of fragmented grains such as sand, silt, or parts of fossils. Conglomerates, sandstones, and siltstones are clastic rocks; the individual clastic grains are termed **clasts**.

Clearance In a natural arch or bridge, the maximum height underneath the bridge.

Colluvium Loose rock and sand deposits brought down to the foot of a slope or cliff by erosion or gravity.

Conglomerate Coarse-grained clastic sedimentary rock formed by cementing of rounded gravel in a matrix of sand.

Creep Slow, downward movement of soil or unconsolidated debris.

Cross-bedding The intersection in horizontal planes of different sedimentary deposits.

Crust The outermost layer of rock comprising the earth's surface.

Deck The flat upper surface in a natural bridge.

Differential Erosion Differences in type and speed of erosion, due to differences in the resistance and hardness of rock.

Fault A fracture in the earth's crust, along which rocks on one side have been displaced relative to rocks on the other side.

Fold A bend or warp in rock bedding.

Gravel Round sedimentary particles coarser than sand.

Headward Erosion Expansion of a valley uphill beyond its original confines, as gullies are created by erosion.

Incised Meander Meandering course of a stream that, over geologic time, erodes all the way through a finger ridge.

Joints Surface fractures, or partings, in rock.

Limestone Sedimentary rock, organic and inorganic in origin, consisting mainly of calcium carbonate.

Lintel The body of rock that caps a span, in a natural arch.

Metamorphic Rock Rock that has been changed from a preexisting rock into a geologically distinct new rock as a result of temperature, pressure, or both, but without the rock's melting in the process.

Natural Bridge Arch-shaped landform, produced by weathering and erosion.

Period Geologic time unit longer than an epoch.

Sandstone Sedimentary rock formed by cementing of sand-sized grains.

Sedimentary Rock Rock formed through the consolidation of loose sediments such as sand, mud, organic material, and marine creatures.

Separation The maximum horizontal distance between a natural arch or bridge and the nearest exposure of similar rocks.

Shale Fine-grained, clastic sedimentary rock formed by the compression mainly of clay. Splits easily into thin slabs parallel to bedding planes.

Span In a natural arch or bridge, the maximum measurable horizontal opening under the arch or bridge.

Syncline A geological feature in which strata are bent in a downward fold.

Talus Broken rock on the sides or at the base of a cliff or slope, the product of mass wasting, weathering, and/or erosion.

Widening of a Joint Erosion causing a joint fracture which can enlarge to form a natural arch lintel.

Window A hole in a fin or narrow ridge, resulting from differential erosion or weathering; also the opening under an arch or natural bridge.

SELECTED REFERENCES

Baker, Howard H., and John Netherton. 1993. *Big South Fork Country*. Nashville, Tenn.: Rutledge Hill Press.

Birdwell, Michael E. 1990. *Coal Mining in the Big South Fork Area of Kentucky and Tennessee*. Cookeville: Tennessee Technological University.

Byrne, James G., et al. 1964. *Soil Survey of the McCreary-Whitley Area, Kentucky*. Soil Conservation Service, U.S. Department of Agriculture. Washington, D.C.: U.S. Government Printing Office.

Coleman, B.; J. A. Smith; and H. R. Duncan. 1999. *Hiking the Big South Fork*. 3d ed. Knoxville: University of Tennessee Press.

Collins, Robert F. 1975. *A History of the Daniel Boone National Forest*. Washington, D.C.: U.S. Forest Service, U.S. Dept. of Agriculture.

Corgan, James X., and John T. Parks. 1979. *The Natural Bridges of Tennessee*. Tennessee Division of Geology Bulletin No. 80. Nashville.

Des Jean, Tom. 1997. Niter mining in the area of the Big South Fork of the Cumberland River. *Tennessee Anthropologist* Vol. 22, No. 2: 225-29.

Des Jean, Tom, and Joseph L. Benthall. 1994. Tentative prehistoric cultural chronology of the Upper Cumberland Plateau. *Tennessee Anthropologist* 19, 2: 115-47.

Dickens, Roy S., Jr. 1976. *Cherokee Prehistory*. Knoxville: University of Tennessee Press.

Gaydos, Michael W. 1982. *Hydrology of Area 17, Eastern Coal Province, Tennessee and Kentucky*. U.S. Geological Survey, Water Resources Investigations, Open File Report 81-1118. Nashville, Tenn.: U.S. Department of the Interior.

Harris, Ann G., and Esther Tuttle. 1990. *Geology of National Parks*. Dubuque, Iowa: Kendall/Hunt Publishing Company.

Howell, Benita J. 1981. *A Survey of Folklife along the Big South Fork of the Cumberland River*. Knoxville: University of Tennessee, Department of Anthropology Report of Investigations.

Hudson, Charles. 1976. *The Southeastern Indians*. Knoxville: University of Tennessee Press.

Levin, Harold L. 1988. *The Earth Through Time*. New York: Holt, Rinehart, and Winston.

Lewis, T. M. N., and M. Kneberg. 1958. *Tribes That Slumber*. Knoxville: University of Tennessee Press.

Luther, Edward T. 1959. *The Coal Reserves of Tennessee*. Division of Geology Bulletin No. 63. Nashville: Tennessee Department of Conservation.

———. 1977. *Our Restless Earth*. Knoxville: University of Tennessee Press.

Manning, Russ. 1993. *The Historic Cumberland Plateau*. Knoxville: University of Tennessee Press.

———. 1994. *Exploring the Big South Fork*. Norris, Tenn.: Mountain Laurel Place.

Manning, Russ, and Sondra Jamieson. 1995. *Trails of the Big South Fork*. Norris, Tenn.: Mountain Laurel Place.

McGrain, Preston. 1983. *The Geological Story of Kentucky*. Kentucky Geological Survey Special Publication 8, Series XI. Lexington: University of Kentucky.

Miller, Robert A. 1974. *The Geologic History of Tennessee*. Division of Geology Bulletin No. 74. Nashville: Tennessee Department of Conservation.

Moore, Harry L. 1994. *A Geologic Trip Across Tennessee by Interstate 40*. Knoxville: The University of Tennessee Press.

Ruchhoft, Robert H. 1986. *Kentucky's Land of the Arches: The Red River Gorge*. Cincinnati, Ohio: Pucelle Press.

Springer, M. E., and J. A. Elder. 1980. *Soils of Tennessee*. Bulletin 596. Nashville: Tennessee Department of Agriculture.

Stearns, Richard G., and Robert M. Mitchum, Jr. 1962. *Pennsylvanian Rocks of the Southern Appalachians*. Division of Geology Report of Investigations No. 14. Nashville: Tennessee Department of Conservation.

Summers, Chuck. 1999. *A Year in the Big South Fork National River and Recreation Area*. Jellico, Tenn.: Contemplative Images.

U.S. Department of Defense. Army Corps of Engineers. N.d. *Big South Fork National River and Recreation Area: Master Plan*, vol. 1. N.p.

———. Nashville District 1976. *Big South Fork National River and Recreation Area: Final Environmental Impact Study*. N.p.

U.S. Department of Defense. Army Corps of Engineers et al. 1969. *Big South Fork: Cumberland River Interagency Field Task Group Report*. Nashville, Tenn.

U.S. Department of the Interior. National Park Service. Big South Fork National River and Recreation Area. *A Guide to the Oscar Blevins Loop Trail*.

INDEX

Stearns, Justus, 21
Stearns Coal and Lumber
    Company, 21–22, 46, 51,
    63, 84

Tennessee Valley Authority, 14
Tension Dome, 7
Terry Cemetery, 10
Thompson Creek, 61–64
Troublesome Creek, 17
Twin Arches/Charit Creek
    Trail, 36

U.S. Army Corps of Engineers,
    12–14, 22, 27
U.S. Forest Service 70–72
U.S. Geological Survey, xvi
U.S. House of Representatives,
    14
U.S. Senate, 14

West Tunnel, 36
Whitley City, Ky., 72
Widening of a joint, 7

Yahoo Falls, 70, 79–81
Yamacraw, 84, 88

The Natural Arches of the Big South Fork was designed and type-set on a Macintosh computer system using PageMaker software. The text is set in Sabon, and the titles are set in Block Heavy. This book was designed by Todd Duren, composed by Kimberly Scarbrough, and manufactured by Thomson-Shore, Inc. The re-cycled paper used in this book is designed for an effective life of at least three hundred years.